My Life After Dying

Becoming Alive to Universal Love

George G. Ritchie, Jr., M.D.

Introduction by Ian Stevenson, M.D.

HR HAMPTONROADS
PUBLISHING COMPANY, INC.

For information, write:

Hampton Roads Publishing Co., Inc.
891 Norfolk Square
Norfolk, VA 23502

Or call: 804-459-2453
    FAX: 804-455-8907

If this book is unavailable from your local bookseller, it may be obtained directly from the publisher. Call toll-free 1-800-766-8009 (orders only).

ISBN 1-878901-25-7

10 9 8 7 6 5 4 3

Printed in the United States of America

Thanks particularly to
Mary Skeen Ritchie,
Marguerite S. Ritchie, and
Dr. John A. Coleman,

also to
Dr. John MacLean,
Rev. Rufus J. Womble,
Dr. A. Purnell Bailey,
Rev. Jesse W. Moore,
Dr. Sidney Crane,
Rev. R. Robert Ismay,
Rev. W. Stewart Maxey,
Dr. Wilmer A. Blankenbaker,
Rev. Tom W. Blair, Jr.,
Rev. John H. Farmer, and
Dr. Ian Stevenson,
all of whom believed in my experiences
and encouraged me in my search for truth
and in learning more about our living Christ.

I also wish to thank
Jane Deringer,
Frank DeMarco,
Bob Friedman and
John F. Dickinson,
who taught, edited, and encouraged me
until this book came into existence.

Contents

Foreword by Ian Stevenson / ix
Introduction / xiii

I.
Review of The Death Experience

Chapter 1 Heading Towards The Beginning or The End? / 2
Chapter 2 Preamble / 8
Chapter 3 Experiencing The Epiphany / 12
Chapter 4 Many Realms / 17

II.
The Valley of Life,
Also A Place to Learn

Chapter 5 From The Mountain into The Valley / 32
Chapter 6 More Training and Discipline / 41
Chapter 7 Cause and Effect / 49
Chapter 8 Spiritual Psychosomatic Medicine / 56
Chapter 9 The Healing of An Alcoholic / 65
Chapter 10 Spiritual Healing, A Part of Medicine / 73
Chapter 11 Understanding Two Different Sexual Orientations / 86

III
Searching For The Truth
That Can Free Us To Live

Chapter 12 You Have To Realize That You Are Dead / 96
Chapter 13 Organized Religion: Is It Following God? / 111
Chapter 14 Who Is Our Leader? Who Is Teaching Us? / 120
Chapter 15 What Is Man / 128
Chapter 16 Our Ultimate Destiny / 136

Notes / 149

Foreword

by Ian Stevenson, M.D.

George Ritchie's request that I introduce this book has made me ask myself what my credentials for writing its foreword are. I have only two, but they are perhaps important for the present purpose. First, I have known George Ritchie for 30 years in several different contexts: as a person who had the experience of being pronounced dead and reviving; as a psychiatric resident training under me; as a colleague psychiatrist, and as a friend for whom I have great respect and affection. My other qualification for introducing this book is that experiences like George Ritchie's when he was near death have been one of my major research interests for more than 30 years.

George Ritchie was in fact one of the first persons with such experiences whom I interviewed when I was beginning to investigate experiences like his. In that connection, I met him first in February, 1962. Since then I have often heard him talk about his experience and have read at least three different accounts of it that he himself has written at separate times. I am therefore in a position to testify that the reports of his experience have not varied in their essentials over the 30-year period during which I have known him. Understandably, some accounts give details that others omit; they were and are, after all, presented to different audiences. There has, however, been no embellishment whatever of George Ritchie's memory of his experiences. I think it important to emphasize the stability of his narration, because so many persons mistakenly believe that accounts of extraordinary experiences always become exaggerated with the passage of time.

During the several decades of my investigations of these experiences, I have interviewed perhaps 100 persons who have had experiences of the same general type as George Ritchie's, and I have probably read written or published accounts of at least 100 other such experiences. George Ritchie's is one of the most detailed narratives of these experiences known to me. He had an unusually rich one, not only because of his seeming flight to Vicksburg, Mississippi, from

Camp Barkeley, Texas, but even more because of his panoramic memory and the remarkable revelations facilitated by the Person he believes is Jesus Christ.

I have a particular interest in the changes that most persons who come close to death and survive say that their experiences have made in their behavior and in their attitude toward death. It is difficult to believe that a single experience, lasting only a few minutes, could radically transform a personality that had seemingly been fixed for many years, and yet it is even more difficult to discredit the assertions by so many patently honest persons that this has indeed happened to them.

George Ritchie tells his readers about the profound change that he underwent as a result of his experience. As I mentioned, he believes that he had a personal meeting with Jesus Christ. More than that, however, he believes that we all have a capacity for a similar experience of Christ within us. We can appeal to Him, and He may answer our petitions. The appeal and the response may extend to seemingly miraculous healings, of which George Ritchie gives us several impressive examples in this book.

Yet we must qualify for the response through our faith in Jesus and through our conduct. Not for George Ritchie is the teaching of many churches that mere conformity to a doctrine and associated rituals will suffice to bring us the assistance of Christ. He does not believe that Jesus' death nullified our sins, but rather that his life gave us an example we must follow — however difficult this may seem — if we are to nullify them ourselves. Fortunately, as we stumble along, we can be sure of the assistance of an infinitely loving God. George Ritchie wants to help us believe, as he does, not in a forgiving God — because that presupposes a judgmental God — but in one of inexhaustible and ever-available love.

It is impossible for most of us to read the teachings of Jesus as described in the four Gospels and other books of the New Testament without thinking that He set standards for our conduct that seem unattainably high. When I labor to remove a few of my own deficiencies, I almost envy George Ritchie the experience he had which, in a few minutes, carried him to a faith and a level of moral superiority that nearly all of us lack. George Ritchie is aware of the great advantage he has had over most of us in being pronounced dead. He does not wish this to happen to any of us, his readers! What he does hope is that others may benefit from reading about his experience. If the experience itself can be marvelously transforming, reading about it can greatly help those of us who do not have the experience. And speaking for myself I know that every time I have listened to George Ritchie narrate his experience, I have felt a surge in my too-feeble wish to make myself a better person. If the readers of this book benefit as much from reading it as I have benefitted from knowing and listening to George Ritchie, they will live a better life and in doing so come to fear death less or not at all.

Introduction

The background knowledge for this book came from four major sources of experiences in life.

The first experiences came as the result of the love, the correct and mistaken concepts, and the discipline I received from my family.

The second was an experience that I went through at 20 years of age when I was serving in the U.S. Army and was pronounced dead. This occurred in December, 1943, while I was confined in the Camp Barkeley Station Hospital with a diagnosis of double lobar pneumonia. Because of the unusual nature and the profound impact of this experience upon my own mental and spiritual growth and its implications for all of us, I have gone into ample detail in chapters one through four to describe what happened and the circumstances under which it happened.

The third source comes as a result of the training and discipline received in the U.S. Army, in medical school and in the hospital training necessary to develop both as a family physician and as a psychiatrist.

Finally, the last source came from my patients and youth, who have allowed me to act as their leader, physician and counselor, and have helped me learn from them and their life experiences.

The ideas, results and conclusions gathered from these happenings in my life are being passed on to you, the reader of this book. When you first look at the table of contents, you might leap to the conclusion that it should have been divided into three books. As you read the book, I believe you will realize that in order to understand the conclusions which I have drawn in the last part, it is necessary for you to be aware of the events of my life recorded in the first two parts.

May this book lead to a better understanding of the nature and love of the Creator of life and some of the things I believe He would have us learn from living on this plane of existence, which we call earth.

Since this book contains information which has been a part of my patients' case histories, the names and backgrounds have been changed to protect their anonymity. Only a scant part of each case history is used to demonstrate a basic truth or principle: The reader should not arrive at the conclusion that therapy is of a short duration or is easy for either the patient or therapist.

I freely admit to harboring severe apprehensions over some of the teachings that are being passed out, in the name of Jesus, the Christ, over the radio, television and too many of our country's fundamental pulpits. I am just as critical of some of our modernist interpretation of the scriptures which would deride the miracles Jesus performed and cause us to believe they can all be explained away by some natural means.

I believe God definitely exists and He is super-naturally natural, as well as He is naturally super-natural. It is my further impression that He has created an extremely orderly universe which operates as a result of definite laws and principles. If we do not make a strenuous effort to understand these, we break ourselves upon them. It is my further conclusion that throughout history God has sent many great religious leaders, philosophers, scientist and teachers to help us to come to know these laws. I feel the greatest leader is the one we know as Jesus from our Christian Bible and the one whom I met in Camp Barkeley, Texas. I further believe God is still communicating His truths to us in many ways today and I hope after you have read this book, you will feel the same way.

People began to learn about my "near death experience" from my speaking in churches and various other organizations, through my first book and the Guidepost magazine article (both Entitled: "Return From Tomorrow") and reference to me by such writers as Raymond Moody M.D., in his book *Life After Life* and Kenneth Ring PhD., in his book *Life at Death.* As a result of all these, a lot of these people began to think I was a very special or very blessed person. I have consistently said to them that I thought the experience happened to me either because I was possibly more spiritually dense than most people, or because the Christ used me and trusted me to share the experience with others.

I do know that ever since the experience, I have carried a terrific sense of urgency to share it with the lonely, discouraged and dis-eased people such as alcoholics, drug addicts and the social outcast. I have shared what I have learned from this and other training experiences with my patients and audiences, the knowledge that a God of love loves us regardless of our race, creed or color. I have received many letters and have had patients say that my sharing my experiences with them has either saved them from committing suicide or has completely turned their life around because it gave them a much better understanding of God's love and plan for their lives. I realize I have had to inject much of my own personal history into this book, but I do so because I hope the reader will come to realize, if God can put up with a "knucklehead" like myself, then He certainly can love and forgive others.

One other point I would like for my readers to recall—life is too complicated to be reduced to the simplicity which most people want to make of it. This is especially true when it comes to understanding the cause of disease. More often the cause of disease is not "either or" but "both and". This is especially true when it comes to the understanding of psychophysiological conditions such as cancer and most of our mental disturbances.

I.

Review of
The Death Experience

Chapter 1

Heading Toward The Beginning, or The End?

September, 1943

What 20-year-old would believe that he would be pronounced dead before the end of the year? Sure, this sort of thing could happen to others, but the human mind's ability to use massive denial is so powerful that I believed when I took out my G.I. insurance I was guaranteed my three score and ten years.

Some very shocking circumstances changed my mind.

In September, 1941, I entered the University of Richmond just outside of Richmond, Virginia, to study pre-medicine. I expected to graduate in 1945, start to the Medical College of Virginia, and receive my degree as a Doctor of Medicine in 1949. After my hospital training, I would go into practice either in my own home town of Richmond, Virginia or possibly with my uncle-in-law Dr. John A. Coleman, who was a family physician in Plant City, Florida. I loved and admired Dr. Coleman . . . In fact, the interest he had shown in me as a child and teen-ager was one reason I had decided to study medicine. The other reason was my desire to help the disabled, for I had grown up with a wonderful, spirited grandfather who, ever since I had known him, had been crippled with severe rheumatoid arthritis.

Thomas à Kempis wrote: "Man proposes but oft-times God disposes," and this certainly turned out to be my case, though I doubt God's will had anything to do with it. Rather, it was Mr. Hitler and the Japanese attack on Pearl Harbor that were to radically change my schedule.

My first hint of the change came when my father, who was too old to be drafted, accepted a commission as a major in the Army. He was in charge of fuel for the U.S. Army camps and would help plan for the storage of fuel for the D-Day invasion of Normandy. Dad, who was one of the two top experts in the United States on coal utilization, worked for the Chesapeake

& Ohio Railroad. The railroad sent him, their top fuel service engineer, as a consultant to any other railroad or large company that was having trouble with the utilization of coal.

After Pearl Harbor, most pre-med students began to go to summer school, in addition to the regular classes, in order to complete as much education as possible before being called into service. By 1943, I had completed most of my courses for a bachelor of science degree. Because I could no longer feel comfortable sitting in college studying when I knew it was a matter of months before my Dad would be sent overseas, I volunteered from inactive army reserve for active duty. I was soon called to active duty and told to report to Camp Lee, Virginia.

After a stay there of two weeks, I was loaded on a train and sent to Camp Barkeley, Texas. It is situated in the Texas panhandle and is the only place I have ever been where I could march in mud up to my ankles and still have dust blowing in my face.

I had almost completed basic training when I was told to report to the top sergeant at regimental headquarters. No one told me why, and I began to wonder if I was facing some sort of court martial. These fears didn't abate when I went into headquarters and saw three other soldiers waiting. The top sergeant told me to take a seat and wait until I was called into the room behind the closed doors that he nodded towards. In fact, my fears mounted even higher when a major stuck his head out of the door and called my name. As soon as I went through the door I automatically snapped to attention because I had never seen that much high army brass in one room. They ranked all the way from the major to a major general. Now I was sure I was in deep trouble. Certainly I had bitched and griped like the rest of the G.I.s going through basic training, but I hadn't gone A.W.O.L. or cussed out any noncoms or officers, and I couldn't think of anything I had done that would deserve a general court-martial, which this must be, to have all this brass here.

Then the questions began. The officers asked me about things I had accomplished as a teen-ager, what I had done in college and in college sports. They were even interested in what fraternity I belonged to. They were most interested in why I had volunteered for active duty. Then they told me that

I was dismissed but that I was to report back to them the next morning at 1000.

During the rest of the day my buddies gave me a hard time. They wanted to know where I had been. When I told them I had been called before regimental headquarters, the rumors really began to fly as they can only in the army.

The next morning, when I was called into the room again, I was immediately given the order, "Stand at Ease." The major general walked up to me, stuck out his hand and said, "Congratulations, soldier, you have been picked under the Army Specialized Training Program to continue your studies of medicine. As soon as your basic training is complete, you will be sent back to your own home town to the Medical College of Virginia to continue the study of medicine."

I thanked them abundantly, snapped to attention, and gave him the best salute I knew. He returned the salute and I was dismissed. As I left, the top Sergeant congratulated me and promised I would receive my orders so that I would have them in adequate time to reach the medical college a good time before the actual classes began.

During the next two weeks my spirits soared, as did my dreams. I was going to be one of the youngest men ever to graduate from the Medical College of Virginia. I wanted to help people, but I dreamed, too, of having a cottage at the beach and owning a Cadillac before I was 35.

My Dad had already been sent overseas, but I would be home in time for Christmas and would get to see my stepmother, sisters, brother and all of my aunts and uncles. This too was very important to me because, during the three months I had been gone, I had missed them greatly.

Ten days before basic was completed, the unexpected happened. A young shave-tail second lieutenant who was giving us a lecture on the firing range made the entire company sit at attention for five minutes because two soldiers were talking. The temperature was five degrees above zero. As a result, of this, at least five percent of our company ended up in the station hospital with an upper respiratory infection.

I was one of that five percent. One week later I was still in the hospital and the regimental sergeant, true to his word, had sent me my orders two days before. They read as follows: "You have your rail tickets enclosed for the train leaving Abilene at 0400 December 20, 1943. A jeep will pick you up at the front door of your ward at 0320 and carry you to the Abilene Station. You should arrive in Richmond in adequate time to report to the Commandant at the Medical College by 1430 on the afternoon of December 22, 1943. You shall be billeted in your own home."

I had shown these orders to the nurses and doctors on the ward. They were a great bunch and all of them were pulling for me. The medical officer in charge of the ward said that if my temperature was down to normal by December 19, there would be no doubt about my catching that train.

On the morning of the 19th my temperature was normal and I was transferred to the recuperation ward. The next morning at 0320, I was to be discharged when the jeep driver came to get me. The night nurse was so nice she even lent me her personal alarm clock.

I continued a hacking cough throughout the day. At supper the guy sitting on the next bed asked me if I would be interested in taking in a movie at the hospital theater with him. I had agreed if we could catch the 7:00 p.m. show so that I could be back and into bed by 9:30 p.m. I was going to have to be up by 3:00 a.m. to be dressed and ready when the jeep driver came to take me into Abilene.

When I returned from the show, I felt a little warm and thought I might be running a fever but I wasn't about to tell anyone on the staff for fear they would put me back into the ward I had just left. This would knock me out of my chances to go to medical school.

I had learned enough in basic training as a medical and surgical technician to know that aspirin and APC tablets would reduce fever, so I told the ward boy that I had a slight headache and asked him to give me six aspirin and three APC tablets so that I would be able to control the headache during my train ride. He gave them to me and I took two aspirin and an APC tablet.

While I was there, I also picked up my G.I. boots, my army overcoat, and my duffel bag, that had been sent over from my company when the orders had been delivered. I placed all of these at the foot of my bed so that I would know where they were and not make a lot of noise and awake the rest of the soldiers when I got up in the middle of the night. I set the alarm clock for 3:00 a.m., climbed into bed and went right to sleep.

I awoke later because of coughing, and turned on the bedside light. It was 1:00 a.m., and I was even more feverish than when I had gone to bed, so I took two more aspirin and my second APC tablet. At 2:00 a.m. I awoke again feeling like I was on fire. I took my last three tablets.

Because I was coughing up so much material and spitting it into a sputum cup on the bedside table, I couldn't go back to sleep. Finally after what seemed like an eternity because I felt so bad, I turned on the bedside light to see if it wasn't time for the alarm to go off. It was 2:50 a.m. But what really caught my attention was the sputum cup being full of blood.

Thoroughly frightened, I jumped out of bed, went into the ward boy's office and asked him for a thermometer to take my temperature. A minute later, when I took the thermometer out of my mouth and showed it to him, it registered 106 degrees. He bolted out of the ward and in two minutes was back with the nurse. She took my temperature, read it, then said to the ward boy, "Get the captain in charge of the three wards."

When he came in, he looked at me, put his stethoscope on my chest and told me to breath through my mouth. A moment later he shouted to the ward boy, "Call for an ambulance to take this soldier to the x-ray section.

While waiting for the ambulance, the doctor called the captain of the x-ray department and told him that he was sending me over and wanted pictures of my chest and the reading on them stat.

"What about me catching my train?", I shouted.

"Forget your train. You are not going anywhere tonight but inside this hospital compound. It will be a long time before you take a train anywhere."

The ambulance men put me on the stretcher, covered me with blankets and carried me out. During the ambulance ride I did all I could to fight back tears. A grown man wasn't supposed to cry—much less a soldier. The chance to be with my family for Christmas had vanished. Was the opportunity to enter medical school also evaporating? I felt so sick, so depressed, that I could hardly keep my senses.

The next thing I realized was that an army captain was standing over me and my stretcher, that had been placed on this x-ray table in front of the x-ray machine.

"Do you think you can stand long enough, soldier, for us to get a picture of your chest?"

"Certainly, Sir."

I got up and walked to the machine.

"Raise your arms over your head and lean forward against that panel. Take a deep breath and hold it."

I heard the machine make a funny whirling sound and the click that followed. Then everything began to go dark.

Faintly I heard the Captain shout to the nurse and the ambulance driver.

"Grab him."

Chapter 2

Preamble

Since I collapsed in front of the x-ray machine at approximately 3:10 a.m. on December 20, 1943, and remained unconscious until the morning of December 24, 1943, what is recorded here has been related to me by other people.

The doctor in charge of the medical ward to which I was carried was Donald G. Francy, M.D. The nurse assigned to my case was 1st. Lieutenant Retta Irvine. Statements by both of these attendants were sent to Mrs. Catherine Marshall when she was writing her book, *To Live Again*. Mrs. Marshall and I tried to locate the other attendants on the case but because 13 years had elapsed and I couldn't remember their names, we were unable to locate the ward attendant or the medical officer who pronounced me dead. Nevertheless, she included my story in the chapter, "Is There Life after Death?"

That morning my condition continued to deteriorate. When the ward enlisted man made his rounds, he could find no vital signs. He quickly summoned the officer of the day, but this medical officer could detect no evidence of respiration, blood pressure or cardiac impulse. He pronounced me dead, and ordered the attendant to prepare my body for the morgue.

The ward boy had to finish his medication rounds before he could carry out the doctor's orders. Then he came back to the little isolation room to which I had been brought. Because I was the same age as he, and because he was having trouble accepting the pronouncement of death on someone as young, the ward boy went back to the officer of the day and told him he thought he had seen my chest move. He asked the medical officer if he wouldn't make up a hypo of adrenalin to have ready to give to me. The medical officer did this and followed the attendant back into my room.

The doctor again checked me for vital signs and found none. When the officer was about to tell the attendant to go ahead and prep me for the morgue this young attendant asked the doctor to please give me the hypo to be sure. Though the doctor was sure of his diagnosis of death, he could see that this young man was having a hard time dealing with my death. For the ward boy's benefit, he plunged the hypo directly into my heart. To his surprise my heart started beating. It was four more days and nights before I regained consciousness.

The doctor knew for a certainty, it had been 8 to 9 minutes between the two times I had been pronounced dead. I'm sure, as an M.D. myself, the doctor must have become very worried, since no one was sure of how long my vital signs had ceased before the ward boy made his rounds. For then, as now, doctors knew the chance of brain damage after five minutes without oxygen to the brain was profound. This is why Dr. Francy made this statement in his notarized statement, *"I, speaking for myself, feel sure that his virtual call from death and return to vigorous health has to be explained in terms of other than natural means."*

Lieutenant Retta Irvine, in her notarized note, says:

"Although fourteen years have elapsed and some of the details are not quite clear, I remember that this patient was pronounced dead at two different times by the Medical Officer who was on duty, yet after he was given an injection into the heart muscle the patient revived and in due time regained his health. During his convalescence Private Ritchie asked me how near dead he had been. When I told him what had happened he said that he thought that he had been dead. Although he did not go into detail he told me that he had an experience that would probably change his life. Even though this experience was most unusual, I did not doubt this man's sincerity either then or now."

There is one other bit of evidence which is extremely important. In the next chapter, I relate that I left my human body and traveled to a city beside a large river before I realized no one could see me. I came down in front of a white, rectangular all-night cafe. There was a front door, flanked by large windows. In one window was a Pabst Blue Ribbon Beer neon sign.

Ten months later, while driving through Vicksburg, Mississippi, on the way from Cincinnati, Ohio to New Orleans, Louisiana, I recognized this same building. The color of the building and the neon sign were the same. The topographical location on the land as it related to the Mississippi River was the same. This removed any possibility of my experience being a delusion or a dream as so many of the skeptics wanted to believe.

Before my turn for the worse began, on the morning of December the 19th, as soon as I had been sent to the recuperation ward, I telegraphed my stepmother so she would be able to meet me in Richmond, Virginia.

On the 21st, when my stepmother found I was not on the train on which I was due to arrive, she became very worried. When she still had not heard anything from me by the morning of the 22nd, she called the Barkeley Station Hospital. After a great deal of trouble the hospital operator located the new ward where I had been placed and got the head nurse on the telephone. When Mother asked why I was still there in the hospital, she was told that I had relapsed into pneumonia, was in critical condition and not expected to live.

The nurse asked Mother if it was possible for her to come to the hospital since my condition was possibly terminal. All of this was an extreme shock to her. Mother told the nurse my father, Major Ritchie, was in England and she could not come because she had two small children, my half-brother Henry who was nine and my half-sister Bruce who was only six and a half and was in bed with virus pneumonia. (My older sister, Mary Jane, had already married and was not living in Richmond.) After suggesting my Mother notify the Commandant at the Medical College of Virginia what had happened, she took Mother's phone number in case they had to reach her.

Seven weeks later when I finally arrived in Richmond and she met me at the station, she was somewhat prepared for how I looked as a result of her phone call to Texas but not totally. When I entered the hospital with the upper respiratory infection, I was finishing my basic training and was in excellent physical condition. I was 6 feet 2 inches tall and weighed 175 pounds. The first time the nurse weighed me a week after my return to consciousness, I weighed 107 pounds.

The doctor who was in charge of my case stated emphatically there was no way that he would sign my discharge until my weight reached 135 pounds. When they were sure there was no brain damage, one of the medical staff called the Medical College of Virginia and found they were saving my place. During the next five weeks, the nurses and ward men

fed me more milk shakes, fruit juices, snacks and extra help-
ings at meals than I had ever had. They were a terrific group
and did everything they could to help me gain weight.

Chapter 3

Experiencing The Epiphany

The night was getting stranger and stranger, I thought. Here I was sitting on the side of the bed; I felt like I just woke up but I did not remember sitting up. What was going on? The last thing I could remember was my standing in front of the x-ray machine. What was I doing in this little room?

Had I missed my train? What time was it? Where was the watch I usually wore on my left arm? I knew it must be night because it was still dark.

The only light in the room was the little bulb in the stalk of the lamp and it was not putting out much light. In fact, it put out so little, I could not see my uniform anywhere in the room.

I knew I had to get out of this place and go to Richmond or I would be A.W.O.L., and if I was, that would be a heck of a way to start to medical school. I had to leave immediately. I didn't have any more time to waste.

With that thought, I walked to the ward hall. The room that I had left was a middle room, for there were rooms on each side. There were three rooms across the hall, the first the doctor's office, next the nurse's office with a wall of filing cabinets. Next to the nurse's office, before you entered the double doors into the big ward, was a ward attendant's office and storage room. I could see out through the glass windows of the double doors. Facing into the connecting corridor was a door, opposite the ward doors, going outside.

As I passed through the ward door a ward man, carrying a covered tray, came toward me.

"Watch where you are going," I said. He acted as though he could neither see nor hear me.

He walked right through me!

This surprised and confused me but I did not have time to stop and mull over it. I had to get to Richmond.

I passed through the outside door and as soon as I did, to my amazement, I found myself approximately five hundred feet above the ground, traveling at a terrific speed. It was a clear night. I was sure, from the position of the North Star, that I was headed in an easterly direction. I could also see the little hills covered with mesquite trees. As I continued to speed eastward they gave way to more pine trees and trees like we had in Virginia. The ground did not seem so desert-like any as it had in the western part of Texas.

From the appearance of the crystal-clear sky and from seeing some ice on the smaller rivers I was crossing, I realized that I should be cold but for some strange reason I did not feel cold. My flying through the night well above the earth without knowing how I was accomplishing this was even more startling but I decided I would take the Scarlett O'Hara approach. I would think about that tomorrow, after I reached Richmond.

Quite a bit of distance later, I saw a large river with a big bridge crossing over it. There was a city located on the eastern banks. I thought I had better slow down, land there, and find if I was going in the right direction to reach Richmond.

I came down closer to the ground when I noticed bright blue color coming from a Pabst Blue Ribbon Beer neon sign in front of a white cafe. It was on the corner of the street ahead of me. I saw a tall, thin man, bundled in a dark overcoat coming up the sidewalk, heading towards the door of this cafe.

I lit down about twelve feet in front of him to ask directions. I had no idea where I was or how far I had traveled.

"What is the name of this city? Do you know where Richmond, Virginia, is and in what direction I should go to get there?"

For the second time that night, here was another man who acted as though he could neither see or hear me.

In fact he also walked right through me.

This was too much.

I went over to lean against the guy wire, the cable coming from the telephone pole and my hand went through it.

I suddenly thought, "What has happened to me? No one can see or hear me. Is this a coincidence that I have bumped into two men with this trouble? If the wardman and this man can not hear or see me, will Mother be able to see or hear me? Will the commandant or any of the professors or students be able to know I am there? What is the use of going on if they can not?

"I have never had to face any problem like this. If I don't continue going where I'm going, wherever that may be, then do I go back? If I do, why and to what? The hospital wardman couldn't see me either.

"What was that covered mound I left in the bed after I stood up back in the room in Texas? Could that have been a body? I don't like this line of thought: A human isn't separated from their body un...less *they are dead!*

"If I am, then what is this thing that I am in now? It can go through doors without opening them. It can fly. It does not feel cold. As remarkable as these qualities are, they are no good to me if I can not be seen. I have to go back to that hospital in Camp Barkeley and get my other body!

"I am too young to die. I'm only 20 years old. I have too many things to do with my life. I *have to get back to that hospital.*"

I had no sooner thought about returning to the hospital when I found myself up in the air and traveling, this time rapidly, in a westerly direction. Before I could adequately take in what was happening to me, I found myself standing in front of the Barkeley Station Hospital.

I had made two other discoveries about this strange out-of-body realm. First, one goes wherever his/her soul's sincere desire leads him/her. Secondly, time in this realm, if it exists at all, is much shorter than our normal human realm, or the capacity to cover great distances in a regular period of time is vastly increased, for the distance I knew I had traveled could not be covered in our fastest airplanes.

I was in trouble now, for when I left the hospital, I was in such a great rush that I had not taken the trouble to look and see which ward I had left. What had happened with the human beings before was still true. These people, the doctors and nurses now, also could not see or hear me and there was no way I could ask them for information about where my room was located. This was a much larger hospital than I had realized since I had been in only two wards and the movie theater. Now I found myself wandering from ward to ward, room to room, trying to find that little room that I had been in before I left.

I could see the nurses, doctors, and ward attendants, but as I have said, they could not see me. I could see the soldiers lying in the beds because I was trying to find my body. I saw several who looked like me but the ones that had their left hand out from under the cover did not have my Phi Gamma Delta fraternity ring on their ring finger. I was becoming increasing discouraged, frightened and feeling alone and separated from the rest of the human race.

I continued to search from ward to ward and room to room.

I had begun to believe I was going to be condemned to spending an eternity doing this when I came into a poorly lit room. It had only a night light on in the stalk of the lamp.

Lying in the bed with a sheet pulled up over the head was this body. When they pulled up the sheet to cover the body, they left the left arm and hand uncovered. *There on the left ring finger was my Phi Gamma Delta and University of Richmond ring with 19 on one side and 45 on the other side of the oval black onyx with the silver owl on front of it.* The onyx even had the chip on the side that had happened when I knocked my hand against something going through the obstacle course.

I did not like the color of the hand because it had the same appearance my grandfather's hand had had three years before when I saw it right after he died. Now my massive denial was breaking down and I was going to have to accept the fact that I was dead.

I could not believe this had happened to me. I was supposed to become the outstanding young doctor. I was going to have a wonderful Christmas with my family after being away so long. I was the one whom my good friends back in college were going to be so glad to see and I was going to be so excited to see them .

Now I would not be able to see any of them again. No, not even my family, whom I now missed so deeply. I could not even communicate with the staff and soldiers I could see in the ward. I have never felt so alone, discouraged and frightened.

"Oh God, where are you when I am so lost and discouraged?"

I could walk through the bed and walls. I could not pick up the sheet when I wanted to pull back the covers to look at the face to make sure it was my body. I could, by a manner of thinking, manage to sit on the bed beside the body.

I had discovered it was impossible to get the spiritual or soul body into or through any of the small openings in the human body. I was fini, caput, at my end, and giving up.

I had been raised a southern Baptist. At eleven years of age I had gone to the country to visit some friends of a family who lived fifteen miles outside of Mineral, Virginia. Their Presbyterian church, The Kirk of the Cliff, was holding a fire-and-brimstone revival. I believe it must have been the last one the Presbyterians held in the state of Virginia.

When I did not join the church the first night, I became so frightened, I joined it the second night. Fortunately, when I returned to Richmond, I was transferred to Ginter Park Presbyterian Church which was only five blocks from where we lived. There I came under the care of one of the finest and most wonderful ministers I have ever known, Dr.John MacLean. I was a member of this church when I joined the service.

I still carried the concept that when one died, he/she slept until judgment day when he/she would be judged and then sent to heaven or hell. The experience I was having now had never been mentioned.

Suddenly an amazing thing began. The light at the end of the bed began to grow brighter and brighter. I first thought it was the little night light until I realized it was coming from beside the white bedside table at the head of the bed. It continued to increase in intensity until it seemed to be equal to a million welders' lights. I knew if I had been seeing through my human eyes instead of those of my spiritual body I would have been blinded.

Then three things happened instantaneously. *Something deep inside of my spiritual being said, "STAND UP. YOU ARE IN THE PRESENCE OF THE SON OF GOD."*

I was suddenly propelled up and off the bed. Out of the brilliant light at the head of the bed stepped the most magnificent Being I have ever known.

The hospital walls disappeared and in the place of them was a living panorama of my entire life where I saw in detail everything I had ever experienced, from my own caesarean birth through my present death.

I was in the presence of the one who said, "I am the Alpha and the Omega who is and who was and who is to come, the sovereign Lord of all".

Chapter 4

Many Realms

The First Realm: Earth

Since the first realm is earth, the place where I had spent 20 years of my life, it would take many books to record everything the panorama recorded. I have only touched upon enough incidents to drive home some points. There will be other times when I shall refer to something I saw at this time or later recalled which helped me arrive at the lessons that I feel are important. All of us try to learn from our past. Because I was granted this review, I feel I had the opportunity to learn these lessons better than most people.

Before I start into a description of some of my experiences in the next four realms let me recall what the great american psychologist and philosopher, William James said about these types of experiences. He said they are ineffable, which means indescribable or beyond expression. This is so because words formed in this realm to describe this realm often are inadequate to describe things which are not of this realm. What are words but things we use to pass an idea from one person to another so we can communicate. It has taken me forty five years since the experience to develop a vocabulary that can begin to express the ideas I hope to get across.

I want the reader to realize that as the Christ and I observed these beings of Earth and the other three realms of this planet, these beings could not see us. They not only could not see us but the beings from one realm could not perceive the beings from another realm. I was made aware of but one realm at a time.

I have placed a name, the name I felt would be the easiest to understand, on the different realms. The world religions and the denominations within a religion have often used different names for the same realms, which has made the task of understanding the realms more difficult for the layman. As an example, I hear my Catholic and Mormon brothers and sisters describing the same realm by entirely different names. I realize how difficult it is for someone who has not had an experience to fully understand the one who did because of the difficulty with semantics, different backgrounds and separate realities. It seems to me it is these three things—semantics, backgrounds and separate realities—which have caused us to develop so many religions and denominations.

Now for my experiences in the first realm:

I was standing in front of this majestic Being, of whom I had been told: *"Stand up, you are in the presence of The Son of God."* I had never seen such a being. He was powerfully built even in His spiritual transfigured body which radiated a brilliant white light. I thought, "No wonder He could walk through a mob and no one would attack Him if His physical body was anything like His magnificent spiritual body." In fact He did not look like any of the paintings I had seen of Him in the stained glass windows of the churches where I had been. This was no sweet gentle Jesus, meek, weak or mild. Here stood a robust male who radiated strength.

Due to the brilliant light emitting from this being it was difficult to make out the color of His hair or eyes but I sensed, more than saw, that He had blue eyes with chestnut-brown hair parted in the middle. He was slightly taller than I, which would place His height at over six feet, two inches. Though He was dressed in a magnificent white robe, his powerful, muscular frame shown through. He was ageless and yet appeared about 35 years of age.

All of the above description is not sufficient to describe the most outstanding thing about Him. Here stood a Being that knew everything I had ever done in my life, for the panorama of my life surrounded us, and yet He totally accepted and loved me. I have never felt such love or compassion. Before He entered the room, I was desperately alone and frightened and could only think about how I could return to my body so I might be able to continue my life on earth. After being in His presence and feeling His love, I never wanted to leave Him again for any reason. Nothing I had, no one I had ever known on earth could make me want to leave Someone who loved and accepted me like this One.

When He spoke, I heard Him in a way different from anyone else. I heard Him from deep within in my own mind. My mind, not my brain, for my human brain, as far as I could understand, was in my head and body lying on the bed, and it still looked just as dead as when I had first come back into the room. The first thought He transferred into my mind was: "What have you done with your life?"

He asked this question in a Socratic sort of way. Certainly not for information for Himself, since He and I both could see my total life here on this earth. It seemed to me He wanted me to see and review my life. Not as I had seen or thought the circumstances surrounding it to have been but as they actually were.

I could see my birth and the death of my own Mother a month later. I could see that I was so tiny my father brought me home in a shoebox he had gotten from my maternal grandfather. A short time later, I could see my sister, Mary Jane, who was almost three years older than I, along with Mrs. Williams, and my grandparents and father, looking at me in the crib.

As I turned, I could see myself growing through the different stages of my early childhood, learning different things from my family, the kids with whom I played, my teachers, aunts, uncles, and grandparents.

Now the scene was changed and I saw a beautiful young lady about 28 years old coming more often into the picture. She visited weekend after weekend in my grandparents' home. She was a friend of Mary Dabney Coleman, my own mother's sister, who had married my favorite uncle-in-law, Dr. John A. Coleman. It was he and my grandfather's suffering from arthritis that motivated my decision to study medicine. My father was rarely at home because he was always traveling for the C.& O. Railroad. When he was at home, although he had dated several other ladies, it was evident he was spending more time with this lady whose name was Mary Skeen. Then I could see their return from Big Stone Gap, Va. where they had been married and I was told Mary Skeen was going to be my new mother.

I could see I was happy because I had always wanted a mother like all my friends. When I saw Miss Williams, the practical nurse, who had been like a mother and cared for my sister and me ever since I had come home from the hospital, I recalled how sad I felt. I could not understand why my dad did not marry Miss Williams. Aunt Louise kept telling me Miss Williams was too old for dad to marry, but I still didn't understand. I also saw me crying myself to sleep every night after Miss Williams left, until my stepmother, whom I now called Mother, took us out to her home in Big Stone Gap. Then I met an entirely new and wonderful family, full of grandparents, aunts, uncles and children whom I later grew to love as my own. Meeting them and being in the mountains for the first time took my mind off my sorrow. By the time I returned to Richmond that summer I was well adjusted.

I felt my stepmother was growing to love me until she had her first child, Henry, my half-brother. Then I saw something different from the way I had recalled it. I had been certain Mother was the one who had changed the most, particularly after the birth of my half-sister, Bruce. The picture of my life showed I had grown jealous of my younger siblings and had become sullen. Then mother had began to change in her attitude.

I had led a pretty normal teen-age life. Sure, I had gone through the usual sexual explorations of childhood and teen-age and these embarrassed me as they flashed into view but they did not shock or surprise my Lord a bit.

I also saw the pictures of my joining the church but this did not carry any more weight in a good direction than the sexual pictures had carried in a bad direction.

Now my attention was called back to Him when He repeated the question. What have you done with your life? I was hoping to divert His attention to what I thought were the outstanding things so He would not notice the times I had done things that I did not want Him to see, like my loosing my temper or blaming others for my failures.

In answer to his question I thought, "I was an Eagle Scout".

I suddenly made a shocking discovery; He was immediately aware of what I thought and that made it impossible to say one thing and think another as most of us do on this plane of our existence. This new discovery showed me that hypocrisy was impossible.

"That glorified you. What have you done with your life?" He asked for the second time.

"I was president of my college fraternity.", I mentally responded.

"What have you done with your life to show Me?"

He was too kind to call to my attention I had been voted president after a lot of my fraternity brothers had been called into service. I knew what He meant, for the question He was really throwing at me was, "What have you done in your life to show the love I taught you to live?"

I hedged again. Had He been at all condemning in His attitude, I would have been petrified with fear. As it was I knew I not only failed if I answered that question truthfully, but my real confusion was that since I had never known this type of love before I met Him, how could I possibly know how to give it out?

"I am too young to die", I thought.

"No one is too young to die, for physical death is only of the body and a temporary doorway to another realm through which you have just passed."

He brought this to a close by shutting off the panorama of my life. He notified me mentally that He wished me to stay close to Him. We left the hospital room by rising straight up through the roof and then we headed over the surface of the Earth at a very rapid speed. I found myself again utterly amazed at our being able to travel in this fashion and full of curiosity as to where we might be heading.

We came over this extremely large city beside a great body of water. As we descended into the heart of the city, I felt that my spiritual eyes must be out of focus. I could see the human beings and the material world, but I could also see other beings without physical bodies, beings like myself, who had bodies but whose bodies were not as dense or thick as the human bodies. They were dispersed amongst the human beings, who also had an electrical field around them.

Suddenly the Christ and I lit on the street outside this tavern and immediately went in, to observe what was happening. From this point to our return to the hospital room, the Christ said nothing but was taking me to different places to observe, learn and form my own conclusions.

I could see the civilians and service personnel having a good time drinking their beer, wine and highballs in the booths and at the bar. I could see the other beings who were experiencing the same difficulty I had had when they went to pick up a drink. Their hands went right through the glasses the same way that mine had gone through the guy wire of the telephone pole. Then they would stand and watch in great anguish. From time to time one of the human beings would become totally intoxicated, which caused the electrical field or aura to separate, starting at the head and going to the feet. When this would happen, one of the less dense beings without the aura would try to beat out the other similar beings getting into the human being through the separated electrical field.

To save words, I shall call this realm and the beings who belonged to this realm *astral*. Though the Lord did not make any explanation, I gathered that these astral beings had become alcoholics when they were living on the earth and had never been able to rid themselves of their addiction while they were human beings. They were still driven by this addiction and the only way they apparently could enjoy feeling intoxicated again was to enter a human's aura. This would profoundly affect my professional life, causing me to spend much time working with alcoholics and other substance-abuse cases.

If only the people who are now calling for the legalization of these extremely addicting drugs could have seen what I saw, they would realize they need to have a better understanding of what happens to us after we pass through death. Human beings become addicted here and if they don't overcome the addiction while they are still alive, the Lord was showing me that this addiction does not stop just because they die.

In fact, this was what Jesus had tried to teach us by repeating the great commandments.[1] We have to be careful of what we grow to love so much that we let it control us, for it can lead us into becoming bound on this Earth to the things that we made into false gods. I was too young and immature to fully understand the implications of these teachings at twenty years of age.

We changed our location and moved to a large plant in the industrial section of this city. The year was 1943. Because of the war effort, most of our larger manufacturing plants were on three shifts, which worked around the clock. I could see humans on the assembly lines and the foremen and other officers. I could also see astral beings standing beside each of them trying to tell them how to do their jobs, but the human beings could neither hear nor see them, just as the ward attendants could not see me.

This time we moved to the suburbs of the city and I could see a young man walking down the sidewalk. Beside him was this being walking, trying to tell him how to dress and what to do with his life but he could neither see nor hear her. I gathered she had been his mother when she was a human.

The Second Realm: Astral, Purgatory?, Terrestrial?

I do not know how to adequately explain what was happening but it appeared we were going deeper and deeper into the astral realm, into an area where it no longer overshadowed our material realm. The astral realm has its own reality of substance to it just as does our earthly realm with all our buildings and things man has constructed. When we first came down into the city I could see the physical city that any of us would see if we were landing at night by a jet airliner. What made me feel as though my vision was out of focus was seeing another city superimposed on our physical city. I came to realize this belonged to these astral beings. In the deepest sense most of the beings of one realm weren't aware of the existence of the other. When I say we were going deeper, I mean we were becoming so much a part of the astral dimension that we too could no longer see the physical beings or our physical material structures.

We were still in the same area where the large city had been visible but all I could see now was the dwelling places where the astral beings lived which were definitely of a less dense material or more ethereal and I had the impression they were more a product of their thoughts than are humans in our realm.

Just as there are areas in our own cities which are divided by ethnic and moral standards so it is, in the astral realm. There were definite areas of this dimension that I would not want to be caught in, just as there are areas in our own towns and cities that we don't feel safe in.

There were two other things distinctly unique about the beings of this realm. Since hypocrisy is impossible because others know your thoughts the minute you think them, they tend to group with the ones who think the same way they do. In our own plane of existence, earth, we have a saying, "Birds of a feather flock together." The main reason that they stick together is because it is too threatening to be with beings with whom you disagree when they know it.

It also seemed the longer a being was in any of these realms, the closer they came in appearance to being around 30 to 35 years of age.

One of the places we observed deep within this realm seemed to be a receiving station. Beings would arrive here oftentimes in a deep hypnotic sleep. I call it hypnotic because I realized they had put themselves in this state by their beliefs. This was during the middle of World War II and I saw many young beings arrive here as a results of their physical death. Here were what I would call angels working with them trying to arouse them and help them realize God is truly a God of the living and that they did not have to lie around sleeping until Gabriel or someone came along blowing on a horn. Maybe this is the realm Jesus referred to as paradise when he spoke to the thief on the cross. As you can see by the multiple titles that I have placed upon it, I do not know what to call it.

The third Realm: Hell

We were in another place where people arrive who had committed suicide out of hatred, jealousy, resentment, bitterness and total disdain for themselves and others. I want to make clear that it was impressed upon me that these were the ones who had the same type of powerful emotions which people who committed murder have. The only difference is they believed because of their religious teaching that committing murder was a worse sin. Their motivation was: "If I can't kill you, I shall kill myself to get even with you."

I am not talking about people who are what we call insane and no longer responsible for their action. Nor am I speaking of people who are dying from a horrible long-suffering illness. I am deeply convinced we have a God of unfathomable love. Jesus says God is so much like Himself that if we have seen Him we have also seen the Father. Since I believe this, I also believe He will judge with love and understanding those who commit suicide for reasons other than the ones emphasized above.

I understood from what I was seeing that these people and the average murderer also are confined in a state where they are given a chance to realize two very important facts. One, you can only kill the physical body, not the soul. Two, that only love, not hate, can only bring themselves and others true happiness. I believe once they fully understand this, they are given the opportunity to continue their spiritual and mental growth.

. We were in another location of this plane. We were standing on a high porch in front of this huge building. What I saw horrified me more than anything I have ever seen in life. Since you could tell what the beings of this place thought, you knew they were filled with hate, deceit, lies, self-righteousness bordering on megalomania, and lewd sexual aggressiveness that were causing them to carry out all kind of abominable acts on each other.

This was breaking the heart of the Son of God standing besides me. Even here were angels trying to get them to change their thoughts. Since they could not admit there were beings greater than themselves, they could not see or hear them. There was no fire and brimstone here; no boxed-in canyons, but something a thousand times worse from my point of view. Here was a place totally devoid of love. This was HELL.

There were beings arguing over some religious or political point, trying to kill the ones who did not agree with them. I thought when I saw this, "No wonder our world is in such a mess and we have had so many tragic religious wars. No wonder this was breaking Christ's heart, the One who came to teach us peace and love." Yes, this place was absent of any other beings, except the angels, who understood what Jesus had incarnated to try to teach us.

The Fourth Realm: Realm of Knowledge, Paradise?, Terrestrial?

It is beyond my capacity to explain how the Lord closed one realm and opened another. It was not a case of our changing location as much as it was a case of the location changing right in front of our vision. If the previous realm evoked horror and irreparable despair, this realm gives hope, joy, and a challenge to keep learning in all fields of knowledge which help us and our fellow beings.

It is this realm which removes forever the concept that we stop learning or progressing in knowledge when we die. I could call this realm the realm of research, or the mental realm or the realm of intellectual, scientific and religious knowledge. All would be correct.

This is the realm where I believe the souls go who have developed the greatest interest in a particular field of life's endeavor, the ones who want to keep on researching and learning more in their particular field. This gives hope to all people who want to keep learning and have established enough wisdom to realize we have just begun to scratch the surface in any field when we are on the Earth's level of development.

Not only we in the fields of education, psychology, psychiatry and neurology, but in all walks of life, have asked ourselves the question, "Where do new ideas come from?" I know not the answer to this from my medical background but it is my belief that I found the answer to this question after The Christ showed me a few things in this realm. From this realm, I learned how stupid our prejudices are in regard to races, creeds or color. I realize he showed me just a few things in this realm as he did in all the others.

As soon as I became aware of this new realm, I found we were located in an area that could best be described as a musical conservatory. The beings here were playing on all the instruments I had seen and quite a few I had never seen. They were making the most beautiful music I have ever heard. Bach, Brahms, Beethoven, Toscanini, all of the great musicians must have been able, in deep meditation, to have listened into this area and brought some of the music back to our own realm.

It seemed to me that this dimension is divided into centers of higher learning. The only things on earth that begin to approach these centers are our most advanced universities and large industrial research centers.

Our method of travel in this realm was the same as it had been in the others, including the Earth. We simply rose up and traveled through the air. Whereas this had startled and amazed me when I first began trying to return to Richmond from Camp Barkeley when I was back on the earth plane, the traveling method had become usual and mundane compared to the other electrifying things he was showing me in each new plane and place.

I had majored in chemistry when I was at the University of Richmond and taken physics but now we were arriving outside an extremely technical complex of buildings that the setting of the picture Star Wars would have been at home in. We entered one of these buildings through an opening that was more like glass rolling back on itself than a door and were immediately in a high vaulted chamber which had at least four floor levels connected by escalator-like stairs.

The walls on the side of the corridor that were on the side of the domed center chamber were transparent at the top and opaque at the bottom; they were of a beautiful deep blue metallic material that was seamless and went into natural curves at the corner. The opposite walls of each of these corridors consisted of a clear substance from the floor to the ceiling that allowed us to observe the work going on in a series of research laboratories on each floor.

In each one of these research laboratories, the beings inside were using instruments I had never seen and could not begin to understand. Not only could I not understand the instruments, I could not begin to comprehend their advanced technical thinking. I picked up an intensity of concentration, dedication and loyalty to their fellow workers that showed a high sense of integrity.

I felt they were far more advanced than most of the beings I had seen on earth in the arts and sciences. I understood that their work was motivated by sincere interest in what they were learning and a desire to help make the universe a better place to live, not money or fame. They were so far advanced in so many ways that it would be like my taking my son, when he was six years of age, to one of the research laboratories at the University of Virginia and expecting him to comprehend what he was seeing.

Years later when I picked up the December, 1952, issue of Life magazine and saw some of the instruments in the second U.S. atomic submarine engine, I had the strange feeing of deja vu until I recalled seeing the very same instrument in one of these labs . . .

Why is it that inventors in different parts of the earth come up with the same ideas about the same time, Ford in America, Bentley in England, Peugeot in France? I believe I was shown the place where those who have already gone before us are doing research and want to help us when we begin to seriously search and turn deep within for answers. I think this is true regardless of our fields of interest. Again we were moving to a new area of study, and lit in front of the largest library I had ever seen. It was bigger than all the buildings in downtown Washington, D.C. put together. It housed the holy books of the universe. One could place all the holy books of this earth in just one room of this library.

The beings here were dressed in brown monkish robes. They were as intent on their studies of the numerous volumes as had been the beings in the other centers of learning that we had visited.

Noticing the color of the dress of these beings made me aware of something. There were no racial color differences, I suddenly realized, in any of the realms which I had been shown.

I became aware that the Christ was watching these souls in their study of the universe's religions and saw he did not judge any of them. They too were not judging the religions which they were studying but were interested in the many different ways the beings of the universe had attempted to come to understand their Creator. I suddenly realized how wrong it was for any of us on earth to judge another's approach to God or to feel we have the only answers. The moment that realization came into my mind it was followed by His thought placed in my mind:

"You are right, for if I, LOVE, be lifted up, I shall draw all men unto Me. If you come to know the Father, you will come to know Me. If you come to know Me you will come to know that LOVE includes all beings regardless of their race, creeds or color."

The Fifth Realm: The Celestial Realm, or Heaven

Again He instructed me to move close to His side and we started traveling through space at an incredible speed. This is the first time we had left this planet. We were now approaching an amazing place, realm, planet or what shall I call it? The only thing I heard when I was growing up which pictured such a place was the song my stepmother use to sing called "The Holy City." In it was described the new Jerusalem. This must have been it, for the light which shown upon its streets was brilliant.

We never actually reached the streets or open places, for while we were only a short distance above the surface, two of these beings who could see us as well as we could see them started towards us.

Now this was surprising because this was the first realm in which the inhabitants could see the Christ and myself. Even more amazing, they exuded light almost as brilliant as the Christ. As the two beings approached us, I could also feel the love flowing from them towards us. The complete joy they showed at seeing the Christ was unmistakable.

Seeing these beings and feeling the joy, peace and happiness which swelled up from them made me feel that here was the place of all places, the top realm of all realms. The beings who inhabited it were full of love. This, I was and am convinced, is heaven. As marvelous as I thought the previous realm was, after glimpsing this new realm we were seeing, I began to understand for the first time what Paul was saying in the 13th Chapter of First Corinthians when he wrote: "If I have the gift of prophecy and can fathom all mysteries and all knowledge, and if I have a faith that can remove mountains, but have not love, I am nothing."[2] I do not infer that the wonderful souls of the fourth realm did not have love because they did but not to the degree that the souls of this realm had reached.

I, of course, wanted to go in to be with these beings but the Christ was already beginning to move us further and further away from them. I was beginning to understand He was taking me back towards the earth. This was something I was feeling, not knowing, because I had no idea from what direction we had come or what direction we should be returning.

Again I would remind the reader, time and space as we know it in our earthly realm is certainly different from these other realms. In what seemed a very short time but an extremely long distance, we were back in front of the hospital at Camp Barkeley. He then led me directly into my hospital room and did a startling thing.

He opened a corridor through time which showed me increasing natural disasters coming upon this earth. There were more and more hurricanes and floods occurring over different areas of our planet. The earth-quakes and volcanoes were increasing. We were becoming more and more selfish and self-righteous. Families were splitting, governments were breaking apart because people were thinking only of themselves. I saw armies marching on the United States from the south and explosions occurring over the entire world that were of a magnitude beyond my capacity to imagine. I realized if they continued, human life as we have known it could not continue to exist.

Suddenly this corridor was closed off and a second corridor started to open through time. At the beginning they appeared very similar but the further the second one unfolded, the more different it became. The planet grew more peaceful. Man and nature both were better. Man was not as critical of himself or others. He was not as destructive of nature and he was beginning to understand what love is. Then we stood at a place in time where we were more like the beings in the fourth and fifth realm. The Lord sent the mental message to me, "It is left to man which direction he shall choose. *I came to this planet to show you through the life I led how to love. Without OUR FATHER you can do nothing, neither could I. I showed you this. You have 45 years.*"

He then gave me orders to return to the human plane and mentally said, *"You have 45 years."* I had no understanding at that moment what he meant by 45 years. One of the reasons I didn't was due to my thinking I did not want Him to leave me. I was getting ready to grab and hug Him close so He could not leave when I began to lose consciousness.

The next thing I remember was looking down at my left hand and seeing my Phi Gamma Delta Ring on my second finger. Again I passed into unconsciousness and remained in it until the morning I opened my human eyes. I was lying there thinking about what had happened when Lieutenant Retta Irvine walked in. She introduced her self and said, "It is good to have you back with us, Private Ritchie."

"What day is this?", I asked

"It is Christmas Eve," she replied.

This was going to be some Christmas, I thought, I was not going to get to be with my Lord on His birthday nor with my family.

II.

The Valley of Life,
Also A Place to Learn

Chapter 5

From The Mountain
Into The Valley

The details of what happened after my recovery and release from the hospital can be found in my first book, *Return From Tomorrow.*[3] Here I shall hit only the high spots to demonstrate that there is another side to this great Teacher. He said, "I am the way; I am the truth and I am life; no one comes to the Father except by Me."[4] He is *life*, and He leads us from our spiritual mountain of transfiguration back into the valley of reality, hardship and disciplinary training as He did His first disciples or pupils. Like His first pupils, all immature Christians think all we have to do is stay on top the mountain and praise God. I had to learn God is love, YES, but I also had to learn He is Truth and LIFE.

Life is hard. I had yet to realize that if I could not recognize God while living in the present, what made me think I would be able to recognize Him in future places?

God wants us to search for truth in every area of life until we find it. This is not only true on the spiritual level but also in the mental and physical levels. Any time we learn a new truth in any field we are drawing closer to God.

It would be nice to say the next 10 months were easy. Nothing could be farther from the truth. Lieutenant Retta Irvine and the entire ward staff did everything they could to get the weight on me.

When I got to Richmond, Mother met me at the train. I was still so weak that when she saw what a struggle I was having carrying my duffel bag, she reached down and helped me.

During the first week of anatomy they gave us a bag of bones to study and I misplaced them one day. When I asked some of my fellow students if they had seen them, they laughed and said that I was carrying them with me.

There was another lesson The Christ had tried to teach me by taking me through part of the Astral Realm and it is, *We bring into existence what we think,* or, as He quoted from Proverbs, *"For as he thinketh in his heart, so is he:"*[5]

I entered medical school believing I was behind my fellow classmates and developed the fear I would never catch up. This thinking interfered with my concentration. The less I was able to concentrate, the further I dropped behind in my studies.

Around the first of August, 1944, the dean of the medical school called me into his office told me that unless I made "As" on my bacteriology and biochemistry courses, I would be taken out of medical school and returned to active duty. These two courses had the reputation of causing more students to fail than any others in the freshman year. This threw me into a panic because it fit right into my stinking thinking.

A month later, after having made a "D" on bacteriology and a "E" on biochemistry, I was called again into the dean's office and told I was being transferred back to my former army post, Camp Barkeley. He said, " I will see to it that you never get back into this medical school or any other as long as I am dean here because you wasted the time of some good student who would have worked hard enough to pass this work."

This made me so angry, I leaned across his desk and pulled him up by his tie with one hand. My other hand was clenched in a fist. I looked him in the eyes and said ,"I *will* return to this medical school, if it has to be over your dead body". With that I turned and walked out.

In the next few months I discovered that when love could not act as a motivating influence, hate and the desire for revenge could.

I then went to see Dr. Sidney Negus, my professor, head of the biochemistry department and Chairman of the Admissions Board of the Medical College of Virginia. I had applied for admission to the medical school before I applied for active duty in the army. Dr. Negus, I felt, had greatly influenced the decision of the board in behalf of my acceptance. Although he had given me the 'F', I knew he was fair. I had told Dr. Negus what the dean said. Regardless of this, he said that if I wanted to re-enter medical school and could regain my full health by the time I was discharged from service, he would again go to bat for me.

After leaving Dr. Negus' office, I went to see the Professor of Bacteriology, who expressed a great deal of sorrow over having to give me the conditional grade and said he also hoped some day I would be returning to medical school.

This was the darkest day of my life. The dreams, the hopes, the ambition to be a doctor, all were shattered. I knew that within two weeks to a month I would be leaving for reassignment to Camp Barkeley, Texas.

The only thing I had to look forward to was going home this evening, for it was my 21st birthday. Mother not only had prepared an excellent meal, but to my surprise she had also asked my girl friend Marguerite to supper. It was a very pleasant occasion in one sense, but extremely heart-breaking in another, for I had to tell the two most important women in my life that I was out of medical school and being reassigned to Texas.

The four months which had expired since my first date with Marguerite were now flashing through my mind. The hope I would get my M.D. degree and then we would be married was now destroyed.

What a hell of a paradox, I thought. Here it is my 21st birthday, when most people's lives are beginning; mine is coming to a close.

I had now lost my profession. The girl I was hoping to marry would certainly never be willing to wait until the war ended because no one knew how long that was going to be. Even if we won in Europe, the way things were going in the Pacific was awful and how would we ever be able to conquer Japan? I was having to leave my family and wondered if I would ever see my dad again. (He was in Normandy.)

The next week to 10 days were happier than I had thought possible under the circumstance. At first, Marguerite and I had considered marriage since this was what so many of our peers had done. I ruled this decision out because I did not feel this was fair to tie her to a man who had no idea when or whether he would be returning. If I did return, how was I going to support her after the war? She had graduated from Westhampton College and was teaching at Glen Allen High School on the outskirts of Richmond. I did not want her to have to support me. For this reason, we agreed not to become engaged. If we saw somebody we wanted to date, we would, but both of us held the belief that what we had going was the real thing. If it was God's will, I would return and somehow we would be married.

I do not remember the color of the sky, whether or not it was raining, or hot or cold. I knew, as I went out of the front door that mid-October, I was depressed. The orders had arrived on Friday the 20th and we were scheduled to leave on Monday morning the 23rd, 1944. Jim, a sophomore medical student, had agreed to drive his car and carry two other students and myself, all of whom had been assigned to Camp Barkeley. The Commandant had been kind enough to give us a week's delay for travel.

My world was collapsing for the second time this year. How could that wonderful, lovable, all-caring Risen Christ whom I had met at Camp Barkeley let such a terrible thing happen to me? Why had He sent me back if I was going to have to live in a world filled with one heartbreaking disappointment after another. One thing I did know, if it got any worse, I did not want to live in it.

As I climbed into the car, one look at the three other student's faces did not cause me to feel things were going to get any better. Jim and one of the other two students had both completed their sophomore year before being ousted. The third student was a tall, gaunt, pale-looking student who had completed his fourth year and was ousted two weeks before he was due to graduate. His case was the most tragic of all. How could they let a guy go all the way through four years of medicine and then bust him out? (Three years later they were to pass a law in Virginia preventing a medical faculty from doing this.) He too was seriously depressed and I doubted if he would try to re-enter medical school.

We spent Monday night in Cincinnati, Ohio, and then drove all day Tuesday arriving in Vicksburg, Mississippi, around 9:00 P.M. While driving down the street the next morning, I could look over on the right and see the Mississippi River. Then I thought, "Something looks very familiar to me." I looked over on the left and there stood the white all-night cafe with the Pabst Blue Ribbon neon sign in the front window. I looked down the river and there was the big bridge crossing the Mississippi, the one I had seen that night I was trying to get back to Richmond.

Now I had tangible proof I was not hallucinating. My Mother had believed me, Dr. John MacLain, my Presbyterian minister, had believed me. Marguerite, and two of my close college friends had, I think, believed me but all three of them left me with the impression that they hoped I would not talk about it. The rest of my acquaintances acted as though I was a candidate for the psychiatric ward when I began to tell them anything about my experience. As a results, I stopped telling anyone.

After three weeks in Camp Barkeley, I was assigned to Camp Rucker, just outside Dothan, Alabama, where the 123rd Evac. Hospital had been formed. It is the first hospital to which a patient is evacuated when he is being sent back from the front lines, thus the name Evac. Hospital. Years later the television program "MASH" ran a series about life in one of these hospitals.

After two months of training with this hospital, we moved out of Camp Rucker on the 23rd of December in a train heading towards Camp Kilmer, New Jersey. The Battle of the Bulge was on and causalities were running high, so that was our most logical destination.

Christmas Eve, 1943, had found me reluctant to be back in this world and feeling very alone in the hospital room at Camp Barkeley. Christmas Eve, 1944, was not any better, for we had spent the entire day and previous night traveling on a troop train. I dropped off to sleep about 1 a.m. Christmas morning only to be awakened around 7 a.m. when I realized we were no longer moving. I raised the shade of the window and looked out to see if we were in a place I could recognize.

To my total surprise I found us parked in the RF&P Railroad yards less than one mile from my home in Richmond, Virginia.

What an irony of fate. I thought, "What have I ever done to deserve this? Here I am one mile from my home at the exact time my little brother and sister would be awaking all excited and ready to rush down stairs to see what Santa Claus had brought and I can not be there to join them."

I would not be able to leave this train to telephone because our troop train movements during the war were so heavily guarded against sabotage.

When we did start moving again, after being there for over an hour, the chaplain came through and led us in some Christmas carols trying to lift our spirits.

Finally, when we had all reached the stage where we felt paralyzed because we had not been able to get any exercise, someone from New Jersey looked out the window and shouted, "We are coming into Camp Kilmer."

A few minutes later we struggled into our gear and dismounted. We were marched off to the barracks and given the chance to unload and get bedded down before they took us to the mess hall. The bright spot of Christmas came when I had the chance to call home after they fed us an excellent Christmas dinner. I was delighted to learn Dad had been returned to the states and was home for Christmas. Since we were told we could have one-day passes, I arranged to meet Dad and Mother in the train station in Washington three days later.

The father that I met in Washington, D.C. on December 27, 1944, looked quite different from the one I had last seen when he came by to visit me at Camp Barkeley in October, 1943, before he headed over seas. His hair that had been black was now salt-and-pepper in appearance and he had aged quite markedly. He had done an outstanding job in France, for he was the one primarily responsible for bringing the peat bogs back into operation after the Germans had flooded them following the D-Day invasion of Normandy. We had only about an hour and a half to spend in the train station, for I had only an eight-hour pass. It was with a heavy heart that I left him and mother standing on the old Union Station platform and headed back to New York City and then Camp Kilmer.

We boarded the S.S. Brazil, our troop ship, in the early morning of New Year's Day, 1945. Because we were the last unit, as soon as we boarded, the ship was pulled away from the pier by tugboats. Shortly thereafter the Statue of Liberty disappeared as we left the mouth of the river and headed into the Atlantic Ocean.

The trip overseas was anything but a pleasure trip. We had hardly left the coast of the U.S. before we were caught up in a storm. It grew steadily worse the further out to sea we moved. As soon as we left the port of New York, we were joined by other ships forming a large convoy. About three days out, German U-Boats began to attack us, and followed us all the way to the coast of France.

We were located on "P" deck, which was right under the captain's deck. The waves were rolling so high the spray was coming in under the outside door to our section. Our ship was throwing Ash Cans, the big explosive devices for sinking submarines, over the side. We were all frightened; no one was speaking because the U-Boats had just sunk one of our ships.

The boy sitting on the bunk above me turned to the boy sitting next to him and said, "Does anyone want to buy a watch cheap?"

This broke the tension and we all began to laugh.

We arrived about 4 A.M., January 16, 1945, in the Port of Le Havre, France. When the fog lifted all we saw was twisted wreckage of ships in the harbor and bombed-out buildings lining the edge. We were the first unit to be unloaded from the ship and were sent to Camp Lucky Strike in what the army nicknamed moving vans. They were large flat-bed trucks with high sides but no tops.

It had snowed the night before we landed. When we marched into these vans we had packed the snow down and this had turned into ice. Because we were packed in so tightly, we could not adequately move our feet. By the time we reached Camp Lucky Strike, outside of St Valery-en-caux, France, several of us had developed frostbite in some of our toes. This was nothing compared to what happened to the rest of our fellow shipmates.

The next day the units that had not been unloaded the first day were unloaded and sent to St.Valery-en-caux by French Forty and Eights.[6] Someone in the Vichy underground[7] threw the switch and sent this train into a siding that ended at the edge of the railroad station. This sent the train hurtling at 45 miles an hour into the side of the station. It was the bloodiest mess I had ever seen. The wreckage killed outright over 50 soldiers, and we were called upon to administer emergency medical treatment to over 160 seriously injured soldiers.

Because none of our hospital supplies had been delivered from the ship, I found myself assisting one of our doctors, a captain, with only a pair of nurse's bandage scissors and a needle and thread a nurse had given me. We had some morphine syrettes that we used on the most seriously injured ones. Most of these soldiers were sent to a station hospital and then back to the United States.

From Camp Lucky Strike we moved to the first place where we became operational. It was an estate called Arnicourt outside of Rathel, France. While we were waiting for our equipment to arrive, we were given one-day passes to go to Rheims. I had talked two buddies into joining me.

This particular morning I had arisen early to write Marguerite a letter before I left. When the weapons carriers arrived that were going to carry us, I climbed into the back of one and took my seat on one side between my two friends noticing there were 12 of us in the carrier. We were waiting for the other carrier to fill when something deep inside of me placed the thought in my mind,

"Get off of this carrier and go write Marguerite a letter."

"This is absolutely ridiculous. I have just written her a letter. I have fought too hard to get this pass into Rheims and besides, what will my friends, whom I have talked into going with me, think?

Again the voice deep within me: "I said, get off and go write Marguerite a letter."

But I wanted to see the Cathedral of Rheims and I ignored the second warning. The third repeat order was so loud in my mind I was afraid my friends could hear it. Looking utterly confused and surprising them when I arose, I tried to make some plausible explanation as I was leaving the truck. If they could not understand, the top sergeant was even more surprised when I handed him my pass.

The young soldier picked by the Sergeant to fill my place took my seat between my two buddies. The carrier had not gone eight miles from the hospital when it hit a land mine that the Germans had planted in the road. It blew the carrier over, instantly killing the soldier who took my place and causing severe injuries to my buddies, sending them to England and then to the United States.

As I came to realize years later after my study and practice of psychiatry, depression dulls our senses and knocks out a sense of gratitude. I was so depressed at this time of my life, that instead of recognizing what the Lord was trying to do for me by discipline and training, I was praying to die.

I was even more angry with God. Why had He let that other soldier take my place and be killed when I wanted to die and he wanted to live? Nothing made sense anymore. I would have committed suicide if I had not remembered what happened to people who commit suicide when they are angry.

A week later I was sitting on a log in a patch of woods behind the chateau and still praying He would let me die when I heard the staff sergeant calling my name. When I answered, he came running over to where I was sitting and said, "Get off your ass, Ritchie, and report to your assigned ward. Our first patients are coming through the receiving ward."[8] God had started to answer my prayer in a most unexpected way.

Chapter 6

More Training and Discipline

As soon as I arrived at my ward, I found I had an Air Force Top Sergeant assigned to me. Because of my past experience with our own outfit's top sergeant, who acted like a little Napoleon and hated anyone who had gone to college, I was all set to dislike him. I also felt the Air Force enlisted men had it easier than we in the regular Army section.

There was something so friendly and engaging about this 21-year-old soldier lying in the bed with his knee bandaged, I found I liked him in spite of the shirt with top sergeant stripes on the sleeves hanging over the head of his bed. When I started talking to him I found a warm, friendly, good-natured guy who did not let the difference in rank bother either of us. I accused him of speaking with a southern accent and he broke into a smile and said, "Yeah, I'm from Eldorado, Arkansas."

I was there as a surgical technician to care for him. I did not know it, but he was there to heal me on a much deeper basis. Since my two friends had been sent to England, I had no close friends at this time in the unit. I was extremely lonely, which had added to my depression.

I was finding that one could not live in the past with a historical Christ. One must have His presence in the present. When I looked at this top sergeant, whose name was Jack Dewy Clark, I saw the Christ looking out of his eyes. Apparently his commanding officer had grown to think a lot of him, for he found the time to visit him at least twice a week the entire time he was in the hospital.

By the time three weeks had passed and Jack was discharged, we had formed a friendship which has lasted over 45 years. The acceptance, understanding and friendship he gave me inspired me to return to medicine and give my life in serving my fellow human beings. I was beginning to realize that a very superior wise being was teaching me things I could never have learned in medical school.

From Rethel, France, on the 28th of March we moved 209 miles deeper into Europe and stopped in Germany at the battle of Cologne. We had located our hospital in a clover field about seven miles from the Rhine River. As we set up our tents, we could see the flames from the burning buildings leaping skyward as it grew dark. When it had grown completely dark we found that our colonel unknowingly had placed us forward of our own front lines.

It was here I learned first-hand that pain and suffering were not limited to any nationality or any side in this war. We were treating American soldiers, wounded and sick German soldiers and displaced persons. As I became more involved with my patients, my own problems seemed to diminish. Our surgical section performed 377 surgical procedures involving the abdomen, thorax, face, amputations and fractures of all kinds during the twenty days we were in operation outside of Cologne.

Our next engagement was the battle for the Ruhr pocket. When it collapsed, on May 2, 1945, we moved to Wuppertal, Germany. There we took over from the Germans the beautiful seven-story Bethesida Lutheran Hospital on top of a long winding hill commanding a marvelous view of Wuppertal.

This was the first time we had been in a building and able to enjoy comfortable quarters since we had arrived in Europe. I had settled myself into a warm cozy room with nice curtains and furniture when orders came for me to join two other technicians and an army doctor, a captain, in a heart-rending assignment.

We were assigned to good living quarters in Mettman, Germany. Our duty was to take charge of a recently liberated German prison camp, Camp Guerreshiem, outside of Mettman and care for its inmates. It was not a Dachau or Buchenwald, for there had been no gas chambers or mass murders. It did have four massive graves containing 1,500 dead Russian soldiers and 1,000 European and British soldiers, who had died from tuberculosis and malnutrition.

The same week that V.E.Day—May 8, 1945—brought an end to hostilities in Europe, it brought an end to over 100 more of the prisoners dying from galloping consumption in our camp. It seemed these men were determined to live until they knew the Allies had won the war and then they gave up and died. I say this because later, when I had returned to the Medical College of Virginia and was working on the cadavers during my freshman year, I never worked on a cadaver in as bad a condition as one of these patients who managed to stay alive until V.E.Day.

Also in this camp were over 200 Russian soldiers and about 100 other nationalities from Europe who managed to live through the war, regardless of the terrible work details and the malnutrition they had been subjected to. I shall never forget one of them for he was the most Christ-like man of anyone whom I have ever met.

He had been a very successful lawyer in Warsaw, Poland, He was married to a beautiful lady and they had five sons. On the fifth day of the nine-day battle for Warsaw, the German S.S. Troops had overrun his neighborhood, come into his home and murdered his wife and five sons right in front of him. Then they had taken him captive and brought him back to Camp Guerreshiem where he had remained until our soldiers liberated the camp. Our Captain made him the camp interpreter since he spoke English and seven other languages fluently.

I nicknamed him "Bill Cody" since he had such a large handle-bar mustache and I could never correctly pronounce his Polish name. In spite of the fact that the Russians were often very discourteous to him and he had to put up with terrible conditions, I never heard him complain. When some of the prisoners would sneak out of the camp to try to get revenge on some of the German civilians, he would tell them it was not right to do this. As much suffering and pain as the S.S. had inflicted upon him, I never heard him curse the Germans or talk badly about them.

Bill and I had grown to be close friends and I asked him one day, "How is it you do not hate the Germans after all they have done to you and your family?" He turned and looked at me and said, "Did not OUR LORD teach us to love our enemies and those who spitefully use us? If I had not tried to followed HIM, I could not have lived through what I have come through."

This hit me right between the eyes, because I knew the Christ was using my friend Bill to speak to me. I was still carrying hate against the dean at the medical school. I could not sleep that night until I said to Christ in my prayers, "Lord forgive me. You are right but I need your help to forgive him, I can not do it."

The next morning when I awoke I felt better than I had in over nine months, and then I realized the hate was gone. Gone, even if I never became a doctor.

Years later Earnest Gordon[9] told about a similar experience with two young British Soldiers in a Japanese prison camp who did not surrender to hate. When he asked them the same question I had asked Bill, one of these young soldiers quoted this poem:

"No one could tell me where my soul might be
I searched for God, but God eluded me
I sought my brother out and found all three
My soul, my God, and all of humanity."

I was learning the hard way that the experience I had at Barkeley, Texas, was now a historical experience, as historical as the experience Saul of Tarsus had on the road to Damascus.[10] Saul had had his mountain-top experience, which started changing his life, but Jesus led him into a wilderness or the valley of life which helped bring about the conversion into Paul. Was He trying to do the same thing to me? If so, what was I supposed to change to? Did I have the right to gripe because God brought me down into the valley of the worst war in recorded history?

After finishing at camp Guerrescheim, I was assigned back to the hospital at Wuppertal, Germany. (My friend Bill Cody decided not to return to his native Poland but to go to Argentina, for I received a card from him soon after he arrived there.)

We were then assigned to the Japanese Theater of Operations and started the long trek through Germany back to Camp Lucky Strike where we would wait to board ship. We came to a place familiar to all the soldiers who had fought in the European Theater of Operations—Remagen, Germany, whose bridge the Germans had not destroyed before our First Army got its troops across the Rhine River.

We were camped in a field beside a body of woods about a mile from the bridge and most of my buddies were off duty and asleep in a ward tent. I was guarding a bunch of German prisoners we had brought with us to help us move the hospital tents and equipment. Suddenly I heard a German 88 missile pass overhead. The motor cut off and it came down, causing a big explosion about 100 yards from where I was standing. As soon as this one lit the colonel shouted to the major to get over to the ammunition dump and let them know that the American ammunition disposal detail was firing the 88 shells into the area which we had moved into the previous evening.

I looked at the German prisoners and they looked back at me. I could see they were wondering what to do next. Another shell exploded 75 yards east of us. My German prisoners took off, running south.

I thought to myself, You jackass, what are you standing here for?

At the same time, I heard the whistling of another shell, the ominous motor cut out, and I knew it was coming down. I hit the ground, praying I would not be killed. The 88 shell hit the corner of the ward tent, eight feet from me, where 32 of our soldiers were sleeping, and drove the tent pole so far into the ground we never saw it again. Fortunately—or was it an act of God?—the shell turned out to be a dud. Had it exploded, we would have all been killed.

This made me think about all the other times I had come through when I should have been killed. A deep sense of destiny and responsibility arose within me. I have carried this sense within me until this day.

We had just arrived at Camp Lucky Strike when I received a week's pass to the United Kingdom. I had been in London for three days and had stopped in a British pub for a beer while I waited for my train to Scotland. A middle-aged Englishman, who appeared run down at the heels, came over to my table and asked if I would buy him a beer. I brought him two and we talked for about half an hour. As I stood to leave and go to the railroad station, he said, "Here, Yank, I want you to have this."

I thanked him, folded the small piece of paper he had given me and stuck it into my Eisenhower Jacket without looking at it. I forgot all about it until an hour later, after I was on the train, when I reached into my pocket to get a cigarette. When I pulled out the pack, the paper fell out. Here is what was written.

To every soul there opens a way and a way and a way.
Some souls grope the high: some souls grope the low.
And in between on the misty flats the rest drift to and fro.
But every soul decides the way that he or she shall go.

These words became more indelibly written into my brain each time I read them until today they are still there. Again I realized God could and did use anyone He wished to speak to us if we would learn to recognize Him. This was to play a part in my decision when I had to decide whether to stay in the army or to go back to medical school.

When I returned to the unit after my pass, I discovered that since V.J. Day had occurred while I was in England, our orders to go to Japan had been canceled. I was ordered to go back to Germany in the army of occupation. I stayed there in a station hospital in Bayreuth, Germany, until I had enough points for discharge.

I was discharged on the 19th of April, 1946, and within two days after arriving home, I had made arrangements to meet Dr. Negus at his office. Dr. Negus was true to his word and backed my being accepted into the Medical College again. The only stipulations placed upon me were that I go to the University of Richmond the summer of '46, pass Organic Chemistry with a "C" average, and repeat the freshman year of medicine.

The dean who had been there had been discharged but I was no longer angry with him. In fact I felt he too might had acted for God. I realized he gave me the greatest challenge I had ever had. He had given me something to fight for and therefore something to live for while I was being trained and disciplined. I was coming to realize it was the backing of my parents, Marguerite, Jack Clark, Bill Cody and the many friends I had made while in service plus many of the hard things I had to live through during the war that helped me mature and change my thinking.

When I returned to the University of Richmond that Summer I made an "A" on organic chemistry both terms and in my freshman year, this time, I made the Dean's List.

My thinking had changed. In fact Mrs. Jones, a beloved instructor in anatomy, told my parents the day I graduated from The Medical College of Virginia that she had never in all of her years of teaching seen a young man change as much. She said the first time I was there I was very idealistic but my feet were entirely off the ground. When I returned I was still a young man with high ideals but I was willing to work for them. Instead of feeling sorry for myself and thinking the other students were smarter than I, I took the attitude, "If those knuckleheads, the sophomore students, could do it, I can too."

The summer I was at the University of Richmond I met a fifteen-year-old boy whose father had died four months before I returned to the United States. He found out I had been an Eagle Scout and asked me if I would go camping with him and his Explorer post. In spite of the fact I had sworn that if I got out of the army, I would never spend another night under canvas, I found myself on this camping trip. Then he asked me to start attending the Explorer Meetings with him. Soon after this weekend I started back to medical school.

Dr. Negus was not only head of the biochemistry department at the medical college but he was also past president of the Boy Scout council of Richmond. I went to see him one day and said, "Do you think I am crazy if I ask you if I can become an assistant Post advisor to this first Explorer post we have here in Richmond?"

He looked at me with his head cocked over and with those keen blue eyes of his and said, "George Ritchie, I have gotten you into this medical school twice, if you bust out of here this time, I am not going to get you in here a third time. *Do I make myself clear?*"

"Yes Sir. I want you to promise me something."

"What is that?"

"If I make the Dean's List while I am running this Explorer post will you promise not to get after me about my scouting activities?"

"Yes!," he answered with more than just a challenge in his eyes.

I had learned that what you really expect to happen in life does. I had learned that if I could live through a war and if I could go back to the University of Richmond and make an "A" on a subject as hard as organic chemistry, I could make the Dean's List. I did. Scouts had meant so much to me as a boy. The fathers of half of the boys in this Explorer post were dead or divorced and I wanted to help the boys as much as my scoutmaster had helped me.

Marguerite had waited for me the whole time I was overseas and upon my return, we started dating again. We wanted to get married as soon as possible but we both decided it would be better to wait a little longer, until I passed my first year of medicine. The summer after my freshman year, I got a job as a camp doctor in a YMCA boys' camp. As soon as it was finished, Marguerite and I were married. Everything I thought I had lost had now been restored and I had learned that the Great Teacher also lives in the valley.

Chapter 7

Cause and Effect

Nature, science, medicine, religion,[11] and the great philosophers of the world have all taught that one cannot plant corn and raise wheat...or, man reaps what he sows. Medicine, as much as any science, drives home this point.

The man speaking at the podium in front of the auditorium of the Egyptian Building of the Medical College of Virginia spoke with a distinct British accent. His eyes were blue, his snow-white hair gave him a distinguished look. He had a noble forehead and clear-cut jaw lines. Yet his appearance was not the most striking thing about Dr. Frank Appleby, Chairman of the Department of Pathology. It was his infectious enthusiasm in searching for the truth that had made him a Rhodes Scholar and one of the most beloved and distinguished members of the staff of the medical college.

He not only made us learn to recognize a class-three carcinoma of the lung when we were looking at the tissue through the microscope: He made us go further. He made us look up the medical case history on the patient to find whether he had smoked or not, long before the average doctor had connected smoking with cancer.

If the patient smoked, how much and what kind of pressure was he under that might have caused him to smoke excessively? Did he/she have an enlarged heart, which might indicate improper exchange of blood to air because the heart was no longer the effective pump it should be? If this was the case, what part did the improper blood/oxygen ratio play in the development of cancer?

Was there a background history of cancer in the family, particularly lung cancer? Where did the patient work? Was he/she exposed to any carcinogenic substance in the air? Dr. Appleby, as much as any man, taught us to look for cause. I feel I learned more physiology from him than I did in the physiology classes.

This morning he made a statement that was electrifying, and challenged my mind.

He said, "Young men, you who would become doctors. Something happens to a human being from the time he is well until the time he becomes clinically sick which is not included in scientific medicine as we know it to day. Human beings do not suddenly become sick. Did you ever stop to think the word disease comes from two words dis (without) and ease (bliss, well being, happiness)? Do not man's thoughts and actions lead to disease?

Dr. Appleby was saying something profound, something we must come to know and understand beyond the intricate scientific courses. He was looking at something deeper, what we let control us. Again I felt I had recognized THE GREAT TEACHER SPEAKING through this outstanding teacher. Five years later, after I had finished my hospital training and gone into general practice, (today called family practice), I had the chance to begin to use Dr. Appleby's advice.

Two months after Marguerite and I were married, we had rented an apartment in the home of my uncle- and aunt-in-law's due to the housing shortage in 1947, and lived there for eight months. While I was going through my hospital training, I heard that this aunt had been operated on for a malignant carcinoma of the breast. Due to the pressure of internship with all of its hospital duties requiring such long hours, I had not seen this aunt for two years. Then she called my office to make an appointment, because she had been referred by her surgeon to me for follow-up care.

When she came in two days later, I was shocked to see her. Both of her breasts had been amputated by radical mastectomies and there was severe swelling in both arms. When my nurse brought her into my office, she never bothered to take a seat but as soon as the nurse closed the door, she pulled off her jacket, blouse and undergarments and in an extremely distressed voice, with tears streaming down her face, she said, "Look at this horrible thing."

I loved this aunt because she had always been very sweet to me and especially so when my wife and I were living with her. I could hardly hold back the tears myself.

Later, in examining the lungs, I realized she had metastases into both lungs and at best had less than six months to live. The surgeon had sent her to me for terminal care. She was going to die and I knew she was in no way prepared for death. She was petrified with fear. I examined the medical records and x-rays the surgeon had sent with her in a sealed envelope. They showed that everything that could be done had been done.

There were only three things I could do for her. Give her terminal care, which included bandaging and medication for pain. Get a good background history, so I might understand what had caused the DIS...EASE, and third, do what I could to help her remove the incapacitating fear.

In taking her history, I recalled that when I was a child, she had lost her second son, who had been born with some kind of mental and physical deformity. I also knew that in all the time my wife and I had lived in the apartment in her home, I had never heard her, my young first cousin, or my uncle mention anything about this child. This struck me as odd and I thought, when I take the family history, I had better look into this. Since she had not been scheduled for anything but an office visit for this appointment and since so much of the time had to be used for changing bandages and writing prescriptions, I would not be able to go into any detailed history on this first visit.

"Is there anything else I can do for you on this visit?", I asked as I was writing her appointment for the next visit.

"Yes, you can tell me how long I have to live."

"That has not been given me to know. I shall do everything I can to help you."

"I can't *die*, I just *can't*. I'm afraid to."

I did what I could to soothe her fears and told her we would get more into her problem when I saw her in two days.

When you get out on the frontiers of human suffering, it throws you right into the arms of God. As I found out, if one does not turn to this higher power available to us from within, then one can end up awfully depressed and bitter. I told my nurse to hold the next appointment and got quiet and silently asked God, "What do I do now?"

Immediately there came into my mind a lady's name, Louise Eggleston.[12] I had heard that she had had amazing results from her healing prayers. She lived in Norfolk, Virginia. I got the telephone operator to get her on the line. I told her about my aunt's cancer and asked if she could come to Richmond to pray for her. She told me a cab was waiting at the door to carry her to the Norfolk airport, where she was to board a plane to California. She was going to be the speaker at a religious retreat. She told me about a book, *Release*,[13] she wanted me to get for my aunt to read, and she gave me the address of a friend of hers in Richmond who had a copy. She said she knew this friend would be glad to lend it to my aunt to read.

When I looked at the address, I saw that this lady lived only a block and a half from my office. I called her and made arrangements to get the book that afternoon after I had finished my office hours. She was a delightful lady who, along with the author of the book, would play a major part in my search into spiritual healing.

I decided I had better read the book before I gave it to my aunt to read to make sure it contained nothing which would harm her. This book and my own experience with the Christ did more to change my life than any other things.

Release is an autobiography of the life of a man who had become a hardened criminal, working for Al Capone. He was captured by the police, jailed and finally put in a dungeon cell in solitary confinement because of his rebellious attitude. While there he was strapped to the side of the cell for 16 days because he would not crawl on the floor and beg for forgiveness from the prison guard. At the end of 16 days, when he still had not given in, he was cut down and thrown on the floor and left to die.

In a state where he was hovering between life and death, the risen Jesus, the Christ, came into the dungeon cell full of forgiving love and started a change in this criminal's life. Later, when the prison officials saw that there was a profound change in him as he began to physically recover, they moved him into the cell with an old lifer who was a modern-day saint. The book demonstrates that the teachings and love of Jesus work even in an impossible place like prison when they are actually practiced. Three years after the experience, just before he was due to be paroled, he was given a vision (which caused him to change his name to Starr Daily) and a new pattern for life.

I was so impressed with the book, I decided if I had to travel half way around the world to meet this man, I would. I did meet him a year later when I went to a religious retreat in Western North Carolina to hear him speak. We became very close friends. Dr. Frank Laubach, who founded the World Literacy Foundation, said he felt that Starr Daily had done more to change the lives of prisoners in this country than any other man he knew. Dr. Glen Clark[14] was so impressed with him that he made him one of his regular speakers at his spiritual retreats. His book profoundly changed the life of my aunt and many others to whom I recommended it.

When my aunt returned to my office two days later and I began to question her about the child she had lost, I hit emotional dynamite. For years, she had carried deep hurt and resentment towards God, because she believed, from her religious background, that God had made this baby the way he was to punish her. When she did grow to love this young child, God had taken him away to punish her even more. She believed that God had sent the breast cancer upon her because she had gotten so angry with him. I felt I had found the very thing that Dr. Appleby was talking about, the true etiology, (cause), of her cancer. *Not God but her beliefs about God and lack of understanding of what the true nature of God is like.*

I explained to her that this sort of malformation which had afflicted her baby occurs a certain number of times in every 100,000 births and that once this has occurred the chance of the child's survival until even five years of age is nil. She had heard that I had almost died when I was in the army but knew none of the details. I told her about my encounter with the risen Christ and helped her to realize that if He could love and accept me, she could not have done anything which God would not forgive.

She asked, "What about the revengeful God of the Old Testament?"

"I am no theologian," I replied. "I do know this, I have seen and been with the Risen Jesus and I know He gets angry with people who take advantage of the sick, the poor, the hungry, and the downtrodden. He got angry particularly with the Pharisees and lawyers at the time he was living who gave the wrong impression of God. I feel he still does with the people and churches today who give the wrong impression of God and keep people from knowing the love He has for us.

"I saw a risen Jesus full of love and He said when He was living on this earth, *If you have seen me you have seen the Father.*[15] If I did not believe God was in the healing business, and is not the one who sends disease, I certainly would not be in the healing profession because I would be going against the will of God.

"Do not forget, this is the same Jesus who wept when He saw his friends Mary and Martha crying over the death of their Brother Lazarus. God is the only one who can truly understand the hurt and anger you felt over what happened to your little baby. He certainly did not cause your cancer. Your mistaken beliefs might have."

When I had finished reading *Release*, I gave the book to my Aunt to read. I then referred her to a wonderful Episcopal minister, Rufus Womble, who, I had heard, taught the love of God. She died five months later because the cancer was so far advanced. But she died at ease, with no fear, because she had come to believe that God loved her and would be with her wherever he went after she left this realm. In the deepest sense, she was healed.

As the years went by, I came across case after case, particularly in my practice of psychiatry, where the patient believed God was responsible for sickness and suffering, and I became more determined to find how this concept crept into the teachings of Christianity. I felt this was as dangerous to physical, mental and spiritual health as any poison could be to our physical health. In fact, I felt it was even more dangerous to our mental and spiritual health because it could make us believe we were separated from the love of God. The belief that God is mean and vengeful, if allowed to transcend death, could affect us in the next realms into which we enter until we were freed from it.

This is what I found in my research:

Hebrew scriptures[16] tend to point to the priesthood's believing that illness was the result of sin. I do not find this surprising when all the primitive religions around them believed the same thing. Priests got their thinking from the priests who came before them or surrounded them.

Jesus did not. He came following the order of prophets, who got their thinking from God. Jesus got His thinking directly from God. There is a vast difference in the thinking of these two sources.

Basil the Great[17] gave six reasons why he thought people suffer. He should have been called Basil the Wrong. Only one, the sixth, made any sense. The one which has done the most damage—that illness was sent by God as punishment for sin—is the same thing the ancient Hebrew priests believed.

"These are the six reasons:

"1.sent by God as discipline to develop character.

"2.sent by God as punishment for sin.

"3.given to those God knows are strong enough to bear it as a model for the weak.

"4.sent to check one's sense of self-importance.

"5.an affliction sent by Satan.

"6.simply the result of poor nutrition or some similar cause."[18]

In this chapter and in the rest of this book, I shall try to drive home not only what the Christ showed me in my Near Death Experience but also the messages which have come through His guidance and training during the 47 years since my return to life.

In this chapter I have pointed out the difference between the teaching of Christ regarding God's attitude towards sickness and disease and those of the Jewish priesthood of His day and age. I can sadly point out that the same difference exists today by people following the thoughts of man instead of the thoughts of Jesus, who said, "If you have seen me, you have seen the Father.... I am not myself the source of the words I speak to you: it is the Father who dwells in me doing his own work."[19]

Chapter 8

Spiritual Psychosomatic Medicine

"Spirit," according to the American Heritage Dictionary, means "the vital principle or animating force traditionally believed to be within living human beings. 2. The soul, considered as departing from the body of a person at death."[20] Psychosomatic means "Of or pertaining to phenomena that are both physiological and psychological. One who experiences bodily symptoms as a result of mental conflict."[21]

From the above definitions, one may conclude that the title of this chapter means the type of medicine that studies the effect of the spirit or soul upon the mental, and of the mental upon the physical body. One might also note that the word soul and spirit are used interchangeably. The spirit or soul is described as "an animating force." Put more simply, the spirit affects the mind and the mind affects the body. We know from our experiences of life that our physical condition affects the mind and that if the mind is disturbed, so is the soul.

Again I wish to recall what I have said in the introduction. The answer to disease is not simple, not either-or but both-and.

We are so marvelously built that our nerves are set up in reflex patterns for our automatic protection and to keep us from being distracted when we are concentrating on something. As an example, if something touches our eye, without thinking we blink. We breath and our heart beats automatically. If we get an infection by a bacteria, we do not have to think, "Now I have to get the white cells of my body together to fight this bug," it happens automatically.

There is another channel where our emotions get in and take control. This is through the limbic system, which runs around the sides of our brain and ends in two little bumps at the base of our brain known as the pyramids. Since I graduated from medical school, a nerve pathway has been found which connects from the pyramids to the anterior pituitary gland. This is the master control gland that works directly or indirectly through our sympathetic and parasympathetic nerve system. The system controls such things as pathetic nerve system. The system controls such things as adrenalin going into our blood stream. The parasympathetic and sympathetic nerve systems control our heart beat; secretion of acid and digestive juices along our intestines; the blood supply to the skin; and the sweat glands of the skin. It controls all reactions not controlled by the automatic reflex pathways or by conscious movement.

The sub-cortex, base of the brain, and cerebellum all play an important role in our vital functions and reflex pathways, as well as controlling most of our body language, which is usually below conscious level. It is this body language that we are taught to observe so closely in psychiatry for it often speaks far greater truths about what we think than our lips do.

Everyone who learns medicine through the study of neurology, anatomy, physiology, pathology and all the other subjects we are required to learn comes to understand how our body works. It is very important for us to remember this knowledge as well as the points I am making in this book.

In this book I am trying to emphasize the part the spirit and soul play in controlling our bodies; this is not taught in medical school. This is not taught in our churches. Our larger seminaries are beginning to require their students to spend at least six weeks or longer working in teaching hospitals to learn some things both about medical and psychiatric treatment. The students and ministers I have talked to have found this most helpful and expressed a wish for even more training. From the doctor's side, we in medicine can learn a lot from the men and women in theology who study how the spiritual gives joy, purpose and a much deeper meaning to our lives. I am trying to go even further and state that, if we are going to fully understand human beings, we have to realize that these three areas—the spiritual, the mental, and the physical—should not be departmentalized. They are like Three In One Oil, which cannot be separated. Neither should we separate them if we are ever to understand what it takes to maintain excellent health. The doctor needs to understand this, as does the minister and the psychiatrist. We not only *live in a universe, we are a universe. The greatest fault of man is that he has not understood this and he keeps making a "diverse." Religion has split us into a diverse and so has medicine and psychiatry with their worship of their own approach instead of seeing the whole.* I am going to give a case demonstrating what can happen when we begin to see this.

A Psychosomatic Healing

I was sitting in my office in the spring of 1954 waiting for my nurse to bring in my next patient. Since the door was open, I couldn't help hearing the conversation occurring between the nurse and a lady whom I figured would be the patient.

She had rapped on the office door rather sharply and the nurse had told her to open the door and come in. She strode across the floor and asked, "Is this the office of young Dr. Ritchie?

"Yes, this is Dr. Ritchie's office," replied my nurse.

She gave her name, address and telephone number and said, "I hope I don't have to wait long here, like I have had to in other doctors' offices because I have a definite appointment at 11:00 a.m."

"As soon as I finish writing down this information on you, we can go right back."

Mrs. Green did not follow my nurse the way most patients would have, but came marching into my office before the nurse. She was a thin, tense, prematurely graying, blue-eyed lady with sharp features.

I arose to pull up the chair beside my desk for her, but discovered she wasn't about to sit down. "So you are the young Dr. Ritchie I've heard so much about," she said sharply. "I have been to every dermatologist in this city. I've even been to Johns Hopkins and quite a few doctors in North Carolina and *no one has done me any good.* I certainly hope you can, young man."

She took off her jacket, threw it on my desk, turned around and pulled up her blouse. "Look," she said.

Her back was a dry, scaly, crinkling, crusty mess. I was not sure whether I was dealing with a psoriasis, an Ichthyosis or a neurogenic dermatitis.

I felt like an old family physician whom I had heard about. A young man came into see him one day with a terrible skin condition for which the good doctor had no diagnosis. He said to the young man, "Have you ever had this condition before?"

"Yes"

"Did you ever see another doctor about it?"

"Yes"

"Did the doctor tell you what was wrong with you?"

"Yes"

"Well, I hate to tell you, but you have the same thing again."

As I examined Mrs. Green, I found myself hoping one of those doctors she had seen previously had told her the diagnosis.

"I've had no peace from this condition for better than three years," Mrs. Green said. "In spite of all the money I have had to pay you doctors and pharmacists, my back has grown steadily worse. I spend half of my nights awake with this itching and burning."

I was mentally trying to review what I had learned regarding dermatology in order to make a diagnosis. You can not treat what you do not know. One of the major things my medical college professors had taught me was to take a good history. I decided that was the best place to start.

Since Mrs. Green had already told me she'd had this condition for better than three years, I asked her to explain, in detail, where she had been living and what was her life situation when the rash first appeared.

She told me she had lived in a small town in central North Carolina, but had given up her home and her work as a librarian to move home into her father's home. He was elderly and felt that after all he had done for her and the excellent education he had paid for, she owed it to him to take care of him in his old age. As he saw it, her husband was dead and there was nothing more important for her to do with her life.

Soon after the move, she developed the itching and burning in her back.

Mrs. Green, who was a spitfire and had a mind of her own, had made a large sacrifice for her father. Instead of appreciating what she had given up for him, he was cranky and demanding. He wanted the entire say-so as to what went on in his home, down to the accounting for the last penny she spent at the grocery store. This had gone over like a lead balloon with this intelligent and fiercely independent female.

Because of the similar personalities of the two, they had had an explosive parting of their ways. Mrs. Green had moved to Richmond. Neither had spoken to the other since she left. She had heard from a friend that her father was threatening to disinherit her. The old man was also developing symptoms that sounded like cancer.

She had given me the clue I was looking for. One of the diagnoses I was trying to rule out was neurogenic dermatitis, a skin condition thought to be primarily caused by one's emotional condition.

I had already had enough medical experience to formulate a practice that I would later refer to as spiritual psychosomatic medicine. John the beloved disciple of Jesus put it so clearly when he said words to this effect, "How can you say you love God whom you have not seen when you do not love the neighbor whom you have?"[22] I knew, as does any other professional who works with people, that our deepest emotions are set loose by those closest to us, such as parents, brothers, sisters, spouses and our children.

The beginning of Mrs. Green's anger with her father coincided with the beginning of her skin trouble. As the interpersonal conditions worsened so did the condition of her back. All of this also occurred at the same time her father was developing symptoms which later were to be diagnosed as cancer.

I was wondering what I might do for this lady when the idea came into my mind, why don't you get her to read Starr Daily's book, *Release*? I said to her, "Mrs. Green, I am going to give you two prescriptions. One will be a low-cost medicine you can fill at the drug store. The prescription is for a quarter grain of phenobarbital. I want you to take a tablet before each meal and at bedtime. The other prescription will be more difficult. I have a book I want you to read."

I wrote down the name of the book and its author on another prescription blank and handed it to her. "You can buy it at the Cokesbury Book Store."

She acted as though she couldn't believe her ears.

"What book?", she asked angrily.

"The one whose name I have just written on this prescription pad sheet."

"I have no intention of reading a book."

"Mrs. Green," I said, "I did not ask you to make this appointment or to come into my office. You came here on your own. You came here because you had been told by someone I could help you. Either you do what I ask and follow my orders or you don't come back. Do I make myself clear? If you do come back I would like to see you in at least two weeks."

She picked up the medical prescription and the notepaper on which I had written the name of the book and stormed out.

Three and a half weeks had passed when the door opened and in walked Mrs. Green. She walked through the waiting room, past my receptionist without speaking and directly into my office. She did not say "good morning" or "pardon my coming in without an appointment"; she pulled up her blouse and said, "Look".

I could hardly believe my eyes. There was normal pink skin all over her entire back. I have never seen such a rapid improvement. I said, "Mrs. Green, what happened to you and where have you been for the last three and a half weeks?"

In her usual shrill voice, but this time with a twinkle in her eye, she said, "Dr. Ritchie, when I left here, I had decided not only were you an inexperienced doctor, but I also decided you were absolutely insane. I felt I had totally wasted my time by coming here to see you. Someone had warned me you would probably give me this book to read. When you gave me the name of the book, *Release*, I was determined I would never set foot in your office again."

At that stage, I was about to explode because some friends of mine had told me that some of my patients that most needed to read *Release* were getting upset because I was giving the book to them. Fortunately I held my tongue and let her continue to talk.

"I got home and that night I was in so much misery from itching and burning, that out of sheer desperation I thought to myself, what the hell have I got to lose? I have spent hundreds of dollars and nothing has improved. His two prescriptions together are not over fifteen dollars. The next day I went down to the Methodist Publishing House (the Cokesbury Book Store) and brought the book *Release*.

After reading the first hundred pages, I decided not only were you crazy but you had a sadistic streak. As you know, all Starr Daily wrote about in the first hundred pages was his terrible life of crime which lead to his being put into prison and then into solitary confinement. Why would you want me to read this story and what did it have to do with my back? Then I came to the experience he had in solitary confinement, where he had been cut down and thrown on to the floor to die after he had turned black all the way to the top of his hips because he couldn't move; where he was hovering between life and death. Where Jesus came into his cell and looked down into his eyes with such love and compassion, he could feel all the hate, all of the bitterness flowing out of him. It was then that I realized something was happening to me."

As Mrs. Green continued to talk, I couldn't help thinking to myself: I wonder how many other people would notice a change in their lives if they could admit to themselves the bitterness they carry around in their hearts.

"Dr. Ritchie, I have been cynical and skeptical and I do not believe in a lot of this religious stuff. I haven't attended church for years and had reached the place where I wasn't even sure there was a God. In spite of my determination not to become emotionally involved with this book, I found that the unfolding story had totally entranced me.

"Several days later, I found I could not read this book fast as I usually read a book, because after Starr Daily had been put in the cell with the Old Lifer, their conversations were really hitting me. If you must know, Dr. Ritchie, I have been holed up in my house with that book by myself for the past three weeks."

Again my thoughts flashed back to Jesus' story of the prodigal son who had to come to face himself before he decided to go back to his father, who totally forgave him and restored him. I was hearing the story of the prodigal daughter.

"When I was almost finished the book, I had a dream or a vision, I'm not sure which. I was lying in the bed awake early one morning thinking about Starr Daily and some of the things he had learned from the Old Lifer, who had more wisdom than anyone I have ever known. I broke into tears as I began to realize all the hate and bitterness I had felt towards my Dad for years.

Suddenly a hand came out of nowhere in the air just above me, reached into my chest and began to pull out something which looked like a tapeworm made out of coral. It even felt rough and tough. The hand kept pulling and pulling it out and the stuff kept on unwinding like a rope. When finally the hand pulled out the last bit, I had lost all the hate, resentment and bitterness towards my Dad."

"Mrs. Green", I said, "This is an amazing thing that has happened to you. You have had a chance to see literally the hand of God or whomever He sent, working directly in your life. I feel that you have done exactly what I was hoping you would do, have your mind become opened by reading *Release* to the cause of your skin condition and then realize the love that God has for both you and your father. Not only have you recognized the cause of your skin condition, for I felt it was a Neurogenic Dermatitis, but you and God have done the most important thing, remove the cause of it. Your back is healing nicely. I would like to see you one more time in one week."

"I can't come then," she said with an amused smile on her face.

"Beyond any shadow of a doubt, you are the most exasperating woman I have ever met," I kidded. "Why can't you?"

"You're a young busybody." She paused and smiled. "If you must know, I'm going to North Carolina to visit my father."

Two and a half weeks after her return, she made an appointment to see me. When she arrived, I had never seen such a change in anyone. The harshness, coldness and bitterness was totally removed from her face and voice. In place of the resentment and defiance in her eyes, there was compassion and tenderness. Her lips, instead of turning down into a sneer at the corners, turned up into a warm smile. Even her clothes had changed. She no longer looked as though she jumped into anything which might be hanging in the closet. She had bought a very stylish suit and wore it with a great deal of pride.

There was a sad side to this story. She had had a wonderful reunion with her father and in the last few months of his life they became the closest of friends. He did have cancer and she spent his last months with him and nursed him because she wanted to. . .not because he dictated it. He really enjoyed having her near and she told me that he died peacefully in his sleep about five months after their reunion.

A short time after his death, the estate was probated and Mrs. Green found she had been left quite wealthy. Mrs. Green was a bright lady who taught library science and had been an outstanding college librarian.

I knew she had been a member of my denomination, and that she had long ago stopped attending any church soon after her mother had died. I looked across the aisle of my church one Sunday morning and there sat Mrs. Green.

She became an outstanding member of our church. Without anyone realizing it, she began to travel, at her own expense, all over the world where we had missionaries. I was told later, by one of the outstanding ministers of our denomination, that she accomplished more working with these people than our paid staff.

This experience convinced me I was on the right track in believing our health is dependent upon three components: the spiritual, the mental and the physical. What affects one is going to affect the other two. When Mrs. Green began to see that God forgave Starr Daily, regardless of his numerous faults, she was open to His forgiving her. She first had to come to acknowledge her anger, resentment and bitterness and want to be rid of them. Then He could remove these traits and without any condemnation. She took the same approach with her father and although he was not healed physically, he was healed mentally and spiritually.

Chapter 9

The Healing of An Alcoholic

W hat the Christ showed me in the second realm concerning addiction and its effect on us even after we die caused me
to become interested in the treatment of alcoholics. As a
result, a year after I went into private family practice, I was
offered a chance to become the physician for one of the two
private alcoholic hospitals in Richmond. I eagerly accepted.
Still later a former alcoholic friend of mine and I had the
chance to buy it out and run it, which we did. I was with this
hospital for better than seven years. I had the opportunity to
learn even more concerning the treatment of alcoholics while
going through the psychiatric residency and thirty years of
experience working with them.

Alcoholics Anonymous[23] is not only a book but an organization run by alcoholics for alcoholics that did as much as the
previous-mentioned training in helping me to understand and
treat them. I felt that when the organized church and
medicine had given up on the alcoholic and acted as though
the alcoholic was beyond God's love and redemption, God
picked two alcoholics, Bill Wilson and an M.D., to show what
God could do through them for themselves and other addicts.
They established the twelve steps of AA and the organization.[24]
Let's look at something Bill Wilson wrote.

"There are, it seems to me, four steps to be taken by one
who is a victim of alcoholism.

First: Have a real desire to quit.

Second: Admit you can't. (This is hardest.)

Third: Ask for His ever-present help.

Four: Accept and acknowledge this help."

The following is a case that will demonstrate some of the
points that Bill Wilson was making.

A phone call had come in around 4:30 p.m. from the nurse
at the hospital, informing me that a new patient had been
admitted and asking if I would come to see the patient as soon
as possible. When I arrived at the sanatorium, I was immedi-

ately escorted to her room. Mrs. Deamer, the patient, was a middle-aged woman, the wife of a prominent minister.

Her husband, who had brought her, had already left because he was disgusted with her behavior. "I hope you can do something to get her straightened out," he had told the nurse. "I certainly haven't been able to make any progress with her."

When I walked into Mrs. Deamer's room, she looked up from the bed. "Who in the hell are you?" she asked in a slurring voice.

"I am Doctor Ritchie, in charge of this hospital. I'm here to treat you and help you become sober."

"You can go to hell. Who said I wanted to get sober? I have no intention of stopping drinking. Did that reverent bastard husband of mine give you such a ridiculous idea? Damn, I know those WCTU[25] women in his church want me to stop drinking but neither he nor they are going to tell me what the hell I can do with my life."

"What you decide to do with your life is your own business," I told her. "But right now I have to get a history and do a physical on you."

In taking her history, I found she had grown up in a middle-class family and had led a relatively normal childhood and adolescence. As a teen-ager, she had developed a nice voice and became a singer in a band. While singing in the band, she met her husband, who was the band leader.

Five years after their marriage, her husband went to hear an evangelist one night. This man must have had a powerful effect upon him because he underwent a tremendous conversion, which later led to his going into the ministry.

Unfortunately, his wife did not have a similar conversion.

Mrs. Deamer finally allowed me to take her blood pressure and to check her ears, nose, throat, heart and lungs. In going over her abdomen, I found her liver was down four finger breadths below her rib cage which let me know she had a very severe alcoholic problem.

"My husband might damn well fool everybody else," Mrs. Deamer said as I was finishing her physical. "But he is hell to live with."

Knowing the propensity of the alcoholic to project their problems and blame everyone else except themselves for their trouble, I asked, "Do you feel this is the major thing that has caused your drinking?"

"Hell no, I like to drink and I didn't marry a damn minister. I married a band leader and this character has gone and gotten all hung up on a myth called Jesus Christ."

"Oh, you are not a Christian?"

"No, I'm not a Christian," she said sullenly, "and if you had Jesus shoved down your throat all the time, you wouldn't be one either—even if you tended to believe in Him, which I don't."

"Is that what is causing you to drink?"

"Damn, Doctor, if I had the answer to that, I wouldn't be here in this damned expensive alcoholic sanatorium or whatever you call this dump."

"Mrs. Deamer, if you don't believe in Jesus, do you believe in God?"

"I don't know, I guess somebody or something had to create this mess."

"Have you ever told Jesus that you don't believe He exists?"

"What kind of a damn nut are you anyway? How can you talk to someone who doesn't exist?"

"Well, I might be a nut but not nutty enough to say that I don't believe in a Person that is as powerful and as well known as The Christ," I said. "I think I would check out and try to see if there is a Christ before I made such a statement."

"And how am I suppose to do that?"

"Well it seems to me if there is such a person, He would answer you if you asked Him. The evidence proving He existed, was crucified and arose from the dead is more substantial than the evidence proving Julius Caesar lived."

"Now how in the hell do you know that?"

"I have read the Bible enough to know He said He would be in us and live in us,"[26] I said sincerely. "If this is true, then He should be able to hear us when we ask Him a question. I suggest that sometime before you go to sleep tonight, if you have the courage and the curiosity, you become quiet, turn your attention deep within and ask if He exists and if He is in you. Ask Him, if He is in you, to let you know some way."

She did not come back cursing this time, "Are you truly insane enough to believe Jesus can live within you?" There was a startled expression on her face. "What are you, a minister?"

"No, but I am a young doctor who believes in Him. When I was 20, I was pronounced dead and met Him and was conducted through four realms of life after death by Him."

"What the hell are you talking about? I might be drunk, but not drunk enough to believe that crap."

"Suit yourself, but I dare you to try what I asked you to do before you go to sleep tonight."

I wrote out the medical orders and told the nurse certain things I wanted done. After replacing the instruments in my medical bag, I headed down the steps and out to the front of the hospital. The nurse quickly followed. "She's quite a woman isn't she?", the nurse said when we reached the front porch. "What prognosis do you give her?"

"Are you referring to her life expectancy or her chances to stop drinking?"

I had asked the nurse this question because I was thinking about Mrs. Deamer's liver being down four finger breadths. With this much swelling in the liver, the over-all prognosis was not good.

"I was thinking more about the chances of her stopping the drinking," replied the nurse.

"With her mental attitude, I seriously doubt she will stop. Mrs. Deamer is drinking to escape facing the hostility she feels toward God because she feels He stole her husband from her. I'm sure she is also eaten up with guilt feelings about being such a failure as a minister's wife. It's hard to play a role when you don't believe in the person for whom you are playing the part. Her husband had the spiritual experience. She didn't, so she doesn't understand it. Can you imagine the pressure and guilt her husband and so many of the congregation are placing upon her? How can one believe in a forgiving, loving God or Jesus when His followers act like they do and how can they love her with the attitude she has shown? There is no simple answer to a situation like this."

My nurse, who was an extremely kind, compassionate, freckled-faced, red-headed girl said, "Well, we'll do everything we can to help her."

She turned and walked back into the hospital.

Driving back to my home, I thought what a waste of time it is to work with these alcoholics who don't even want to stop drinking. When would I ever learn you couldn't help people until they wanted help!

At this time I had been working at the sanatorium for a little over four years. It seemed to me that the recovery rate was about 5%. Sometimes it was four or five months before the patient returned and occasionally a whole year but sooner or later most did return. I felt particularly pessimistic about Mrs. Deamer because she had let me know she did not want to stop drinking. She considered her husband to be a phony and she didn't like living with a "damn phony."

Since I had a great number of house calls the next morning, I didn't arrive at the sanatorium until after lunch. Mrs. Deamer was the last patient I planned to see, for I felt I was wasting my time. With our method of treatment I knew she would be sober, but even in a state of sobriety there was no reason to expect her to be any more cooperative than she had been the day before. She was there because her husband wanted her there, not because she wanted help.

When I stuck my head in the door, Mrs. Deamer said, "Come right in, doctor, I had been hoping you would come by today." She could tell, by the shocked and startled expression on my face, that I was surprised. She laughed and said, "You didn't expect to find me like this, did you?"

In no way was I prepared for the shock I received when I walked into her room. Her hostility was gone. Even her face appeared younger. Now, past experience had taught me that patients say things they don't mean when they are intoxicated but there was a change here that couldn't be accounted for on that basis. It was natural for the ruddy and puffy appearance to be gone, since she was no longer loaded with beer and whiskey. But the look in her dark blue eyes had changed to an amazing degree and there was an entirely different expression in her eyes. She had of course made an attempt to straighten out her long blond hair, as all the women did. There was more to the change in her appearance than anything I could definitely put my finger on.

"No, Mrs. Deamer, in my wildest imagination I had no idea you would be in this mood, I expected you to be your usual obnoxious self."

Even though I had said this with humor in my voice, it hurt her and she broke into tears. I went over to the bed and put my hand on her shoulder at which time she reached up and put her hand into mine. "I truly deserved it," she said.

"Mrs. Deamer, what has happened to you? You aren't the same person I left here yesterday. Your being sober doesn't explain what I'm seeing and hearing."

Again she burst into tears. After a while she related the following:

"Dr. Ritchie, I admit I was intoxicated when you were here yesterday afternoon. I guess the gist of our conversation sobered me enough to hear the challenge you gave me before you left. As soon as you left, the nurse began to give me the whiskey with the stuff that makes you throw up. By 11 p.m., I had thrown up everything and was sober as a judge. As that nice red-headed nurse was going off duty, I asked her if I could ask her one question. She said, 'yes,' and I told her about what you had said about your dying when you were 20 years old and I asked her if it could possibly be true. She told me it was definitely true and was a well-documented medical fact. She then asked if there was anything else I wanted and when I said, 'no', she went out with a quizzical expression on her face.

"I couldn't go to sleep. I remembered you had said, 'If you don't believe in Jesus, why don't you ask Him whether or not He is inside of you. I believe He lives inside of us.' I was thinking that you were the most ridiculous man in your thinking I had ever heard. You gave me a challenge and I decided to accept it just to prove you wrong. I said to myself, 'I don't believe you are in me but if you are, let me know it in some way.'

"I was not ready for what happened next. I was suddenly aware of a great sense of inward peace and a feeling of great love surrounding me. I know you are going to say I was hallucinating, Dr. Ritchie, but I saw a form in front of me and heard this form say, 'I am Jesus, the Christ, whom Dr. Ritchie referred to. I do love you and care for you. I understand what has happened to you because your husband has been seeking me. You have not. One can not drag or push anyone into the kingdom. I come to anyone who truly seeks me.'

"When He said these things, I felt all the fear and guilt about what a terrible minister's wife I had been go out of me. I realized He understood and forgave and loved me. I don't understand it. I know I told you yesterday I had no intention to stop drinking, now I have no desire to drink."

This time, I was at an utter loss for words. I had seen and treated too many alcoholics to be fooled by most of them. I could recognize when they were trying to pull the wool over my eyes. I did not have the impression Mrs. Deamer was fooling, for she had a peace and serenity you do not find in a patient in the second day of treatment. The exact opposite is true if they had been drinking as long as this woman had. You had to be on the lookout for *delirium tremens,* i.e. when they are tight, tense and on the verge of becoming psychotic. The remorse which most alcoholics feel when they begin to sober up was not present in Mrs. Deamer. Even more amazing was the absence of her desire for a drink.

As I have learned from so many cases, most alcoholics are trying to escape from some real or imagined fear in their lives, or some past action they are afraid they can't keep hidden. I also came to know another important point: They are trying to find something that will fill a deep spiritual need. They are not conscious of this and keep looking for something or someone who will accept and love them as they are. This is because they carry such deep feelings of guilt over their past actions and failure that they can't love themselves and really don't believe anyone else can. This puts them into a chronic state of depression. Then they keep drinking spirits down, trying to keep spirits up. But alcohol itself is a depressive agent, particularly in high doses and thus you have the vicious cycle set up.

Mrs. Deamer found the thing for which she had been searching unconsciously. She found forgiveness for failing to play a role she could never fulfill without God's help, the role of being a minister's wife. After treating quite a few minister's wives and listening to a lot of church members, I'm not even sure one can fulfill that role *with* God's help!

She had found Someone who did accept her as she was and love her and help her change because she discovered He was on the inside.

Within four days, Mrs. Deamer completed her treatment. She called her husband and told him she was ready for discharge. He completely doubted this, for when he came to take her home, he said to the nurse, "How long do you think it will be before she is back here drunk again?"

His statement was understandable when he told the nurse how many other places Mrs. Deamer had been treated before being brought to this sanatorium.

Six months later, I received the nicest letter from Mrs. Deamer thanking me for the challenge I had given her, and for sharing the story of my death experience with her. She said it led to the experience which had completely changed her life. She stated she still had no desire to drink.

When I left Richmond to start my residency in psychiatry, seven years later, she was still sober. I knew this to be so, for I had friends in the section of the state where she lived. When I would see them, without them knowing why, I would always ask about the minister and his wife. They often remarked about what wonderful people they were and how much his wife has meant to him and the entire congregation.

Chapter 10

Spiritual Healing, A Part of Medicine

Over the centuries, medicine men, physicians, doctors, or whatever one wished to call the men and women engaged in caring for the sick, have been known for two outstanding qualities. First they were specialists in dis...ease. Secondly, they were healers. For the most part their healing has been limited to healing through the giving of medicine, (thus the name medicine men). In more recent years, surgery, radiation, physiotherapy, psychotherapy, biofeedback, and hypnosis have been added.

For the first time since the beginning of the second century, with a few rare exceptions, interest in spiritual healing[27] returned in the latter part of the 1900s. Mary Baker Eddy started The Christian Science Religion, a religion greatly interested in spiritual healing. Close on its heels followed the Pentecostal and The Assemblies of God denominations. In the earlier part of the twentieth century, Alexis Carrel M.D.,[28] the famous surgeon and holder of the Nobel Prize, and Dr. Alfred Price, the episcopal priest who helped establish the International Healing Order of St Luke, were both active in helping us realize the part that spirituality plays in healing the body.

Edgar Cayce founded a hospital at Virginia Beach, Virginia, which was deeply interested in spiritual healing. It later evolved into The Association for Research and Enlightenment, which has brought people from all over the world to the Beach who are interested in healings of all kinds. It was here that I had the pleasure of meeting Dr. Bernard Brad of McGill University in Canada, who was doing double-blind research on spiritual healings with laboratory animals and definitely proved that some people had healing in their touch.

One cannot look into spiritual healing in this century without the names of Dr. Albert E. Day and Olga and Ambrose Worrall[29] of Baltimore coming to mind.

Next arises the name of Dr. Ian Stevenson, who was Chairman of the Department Of Psychiatry and Neurology at the University of Virginia. He was one of the first men in highly scientific and medical circles who had the courage to look into spiritual healings rather than write them off as foolishness. He did a great deal of research on healings that took place under the Worralls and found them to be authentic.

Bernie Siegel, Author of the excellent book, *Love, Medicine and Miracles,* has long been interested in spiritual healing and I feel has brought us great insight as to how some miracles come about.

I was thrust into developing an interest in this field of spiritual healing by three most unusual cases. I make no claims of responsibility for the healings that resulted in any of these cases because I was reluctant in at least two of the cases to become involved, because of the medical-legal implications. I do feel that I was pushed by the guidance of THE HOLY SPIRIT in all three of these cases and from them I learned that The Risen Christ is as active in healing today as He was two thousand years ago when His requirements of faith are met.

The Amazing Case of Mary Sue

My wife and I had gone out to Western North Carolina because we had learned that Starr Daily, who wrote *Release,* would be speaking at a spiritual retreat located outside of Hendersonville, N.C. It was being held in a beautiful mountain setting beside a clear lake that reflected the blue of the sky in an Episcopal camp known as Camp Kanooga. The serenity of this place made it ideal for a spiritual retreat. This retreat was sponsored by the Western North Carolina C.F.O., a group that was part of the Camp Farthest Out movement founded by Glenn Clark,[30] one of the great teachers of prayer and meditation from 1930-1970. This retreat had Starr Daily and Dr. J. Rufus Mosley, two outstandingly spiritual men who taught you how to pray and to believe that your prayers would be answered. As a result of attending this retreat our faith had been raised to the point where my wife and I both came back spiritually renewed and believing that with God all things were possible.

October 1953, about a month after we had returned from The
Western North Carolina C.F.O. Since my nurse-receptionist
had been out sick for a few days, Marguerite was filling her
place. The young mother who came in the office door this
particular morning turned out to be a former senior student
of hers.

As soon as Mary Sue recognized my wife her face lit up.
Both of them were happy to have found each other after more
than six years. The joy was short-lived, however, when Mary
Sue came back to my consultation room and began to tell me
the reason for her visit. The precious and beautiful little baby
girl whom she was holding in her arms was her first and only
child. The history the mother gave stated that the baby had
not moved either leg since her birth.

I asked Marguerite to come into my office and take the baby
back into one of the examining rooms where I would do a
physical on her. In the interim, I asked the mother to wait in
the reception room until I finished the examination.

I found on the examination of the baby's legs that she had
a total flaccid paralysis of both legs. My worst fears were
confirmed, for this meant the child had been paralyzed in both
legs since birth. What I did not know was the cause of the
paralysis though I knew something had to have severely
damaged the spinal cord. My guess was either damage to the
spinal column during the delivery or, just as bad, a tumorous
growth that would have severed the nerve pathway to the legs
in the cord.

With a great deal of compassion, I explained to Marguerite
that this baby was totally paralyzed and, from a human point
of view, would never be able to walk. For some unexplainable
reason, I felt compelled to ask Marguerite if she would join me
in prayer for the total and absolute healing of this baby.
Marguerite did. I don't remember the prayer; I don't think
exactly what I said was the important thing. What I do feel
was important is the fact that I was willing to follow the
compulsion I felt from deep within and that Marguerite and
I both joined together in prayer, believing the promise we had
been taught at the spiritual retreat. This was Jesus' promise[31]
that where two or more are gathered together in my name
asking that something would be done—in this case the healing
of this baby—it would be done. After this I felt guided to go

out and tell Mary Sue the baby would ultimately be all right, but I would like to see the baby again in a month.

I could scarcely believe my own lips as they were saying this to the mother.

Mary Sue took her baby and left. You know good and well, I thought, this child has a flaccid paralysis. You know that no case of this kind had been healed and yet you left yourself totally open for a lawsuit. Don't you realize the immensity of the medical-legal problem you put yourself in?

I didn't have to wait long for my fears to come upon me because within three weeks, Mary Sue came storming back without an appointment. The first thing that she said after almost knocking my door down with anger as she came in was, "Dr. Ritchie, I am going to sue you for the maltreatment of my daughter."

"What have I done?" I asked.

"You led me to believe that my daughter was going to be all right. When my daughter did not get any better, but grew steadily weaker, I took her to the pediatric clinic at M.C.V. where they examined her and ordered an x-ray, which is what you should have done. They informed me, after all the x-ray studies of the spinal cord, that my daughter has an astrocytoma of the spinal cord that they say started while she was in the womb. It has grown to the place where the spinal cord has now been severed and probably was before she was born. They give her at best only two to six months to live and you told me that she was going to be OK."

Quite reasonably, she was angry and, looking at it from her point of view, I didn't blame her. I was terrified. I had only been in practice for a year and a half and was deeply in debt because I had had to borrow every cent I could borrow to build my home and office and equip my office. Here I was being threatened with a lawsuit that could not only throw me into bankruptcy but ruin any future I had in medicine.

In my desperation I did the only thing I had learned to do over the last ten years when I had been in serious trouble, turn deep within myself and ask, "God what do I do now?" What came into my mind I am sure was even more startling to me than it was to Mary Sue when I shouted out to her what I was told to say.

"If you have any faith in your God, Your baby's creator, you

*will drop to your knees and ask Him to forgive you because He
would have healed your child if you had believed that He
would. He still will. If you persist in this disbelief and anger,
your child will die of cancer.*"

To my amazement, she dropped on the floor in front of me
on her knees and in a loud, sobbing voice, with tears streaming
down her face asked God to forgive her. There was no one else
in the office at the time, since my nurse was out to lunch. I
found myself helping her up and saying to her that Marguerite
and I would continue to back her in prayers for her daughter's
total healing.

I couldn't say that my faith was so strong that I didn't still
carry some fear even as she went out, but deep inside I
believed that Mary Sue's daughter was going to be all right. I
certainly had seen the most astounding change taking place
in Mary Sue, for all of her anger and fear was gone and she
seemed to feel her baby was going to get well.

Two or three weeks had passed when Mary Sue came into
the office, again without an appointment. As soon as I could
clear an examining room, she brought her baby back and laid
her on the table. I stood there hardly able to believe what I
was seeing: This infant was moving her legs, kicking them up
and down. This time our eyes were full of tears but they were
tears of joy and thanksgiving unto God.

I followed this baby until she was about seven or eight years
of age. When I left Richmond in 1964 to specialize in
psychiatry, as far as I am able to recall, she was still well.

A Modern Lazarus

Edlow and Mary Bugg had been friends of our family
through three generations, for my Grandfather, F. W. Dabney,
had taken Edlow into business with him and together they
had started Dabney and Bugg Furniture Store. The Bugg
daughters and my sister and I were friends and went through
high school together. Mary Bugg, Marguerite and I had all
gone to another C.F.O. Camp together.

It was a short time after this camp that we heard, through
Mother and Dad, that Edlow had been feeling bad. He had
gone to see their local internist and they had found that he
had cancer of the stomach that had metastasized. The prog-

nosis was extremely poor, with a life expectancy of only six months.

Around the last of August, I received a telephone call. It was Mary Bugg. She asked if I could come to her home immediately. Edlow had suddenly taken a turn for the worse.

I explained to Mary that because Edlow was under the care of the internist, medical ethics dictated that she should call him and I should not enter the case. She replied, "I'm not asking you to come as a doctor. I'm asking you to come as a friend, to pray for Edlow, for I am afraid he is about to die."

As I pulled up in front of her home, Mary opened her front screen door and hollered, "Hurry, George, I think Edlow is dying."

Mary proved to be right, for as I rushed into the home, I heard death rattles coming from the library, a room that had been converted into a downstairs bedroom. Edlow was lying on a twin bed against the far wall, with only his pajamas bottoms on, due to the August heat. He had already developed a dark red, mottled color to his skin over his upper chest, neck and face and, as I walked through the door, he took his last gasp of air. Then there was total silence as his eyes turned up to the top of his head. His mouth drooped open. I could see there was no further movement of his chest.

I put my instrument bag down on the empty twin bed, took out my stethoscope and blood pressure instrument and listened to his chest. There was no sound of either respiration or heart beat. I then took his blood pressure and it registered zero. I turned to Mary who was now standing at the foot between the two beds and said as gently as I could, "Mary, Edlow has expired."

"Aren't you going to pray for him?"

"Mary. I don't think you understood me, *Edlow is dead.*"

"George, *I asked you to come over here and pray for Edlow*".

Now, I realized what a shock this was to Mary, and that she was using massive denial. She stood at the foot of the two beds. It was obvious she had no intention of moving until I prayed for Edlow. I was trapped between the two beds with Mary blocking the only way out.

What was I going to do? How do you pray in a situation of this kind? I was not Jesus and this was not Lazarus lying here in this bed! I did the only thing that I knew left to do. In a loud voice I said, "Let's bow our heads and close our eyes."

Under my breath I said silently, "Lord I don't know how to pray in a situation of this kind. What do I do now?"

As clearly as anything that ever came into my human ears, there came into my mind a voice deep within me saying, "You are to call Edlow by his first name and tell him to sit up."

I had never heard of doing anything like this, but then what was the use of asking the Lord a question if I was not prepared to follow His orders? With great apprehension, and trying to summons the most commanding voice I could, I said, *"Edlow, sit up!"*

Whether I opened my eyes first or whether hearing a movement on the bed caused me to open my eyes, I do not know, but I was completely unprepared for what took place right in front of me. Edlow started to breathe. His color started to return to normal. He sat up, swung both of his feet over the side of the bed, opened his eyes, looked directly at Mary and asked for a drink of water. He looked at me, puzzled, and wanted to know when I got there.

I found myself thinking this couldn't be happening, but it was. I reached over and picked up Edlow's wrist to take his pulse and found a normal pulse. I then grabbed my stethoscope and listened to his chest and found a normal beating heart and regular breath sounds, though slightly increased in frequency. I looked at Mary and she was smiling with tears streaming down her face. The only sensation I was aware of, besides joy and awe, was my hair standing straight out on the back of my neck.

I knew exactly how those first-century disciples felt as Dr. Luke noted in his Book of Acts.[32] He recorded that they had enough faith to pray for Peter's release from prison, but not enough faith to believe their eyes when the results of their prayer, the liberated Peter, arrived in person outside the door of the place where they were praying. They thought that it was his ghost.

Mary now insisted that Edlow be placed in my care and the other doctor who had been handling the case was gentlemanly enough to agree to this transfer.

Until that Saturday afternoon his medical record showed that he was requiring a quarter-grain of morphine every three hours to control the pain. He lived for another month, during which time he was free of pain until the day before he died, when he had to have two quarter-grain codeine tablets.

Unfortunately, Edlow continued to worry about his business because he had always been a driver and could not come
home and leave the business worry at the office. His extended
illness caused him to become depressed and worry even more,
in spite of the fact that both Mary and I tried to assure him
his employees were carrying on very well. It is my personal
feeling that this was his undoing; I believe if he had had
Mary's faith he would have completely recovered.

Edlow died in his sleep one night. By this time both he and
Mary were better acclimated to his ultimately leaving. I had
seen a miracle take place—I'm afraid in spite of me rather
than because of me. I believe Jesus would have said to Mary
the same thing that He said about the Roman Centurion, *I
tell you, nowhere, even in Israel, have I found faith like this.*[33]

The Healing of Malignant Hypertension

I had known Frank socially. He lived in the Western section
of Henrico County, where I was located, but I had never had
him as a patient. He was what today we would call an
entrepreneur in his field of advertizing, with the capacity to
develop new ideas and the energy to carry them through. He
had an outgoing personality and a terrific sense of humor. In
fact everything was going fine for Frank, for he also had a
wonderful wife and teen-age son.

That is, everything was going fine until Frank began to
suffer from severe headaches. One night, when a headache
had become so severe that he could no longer stand it, he went
to the emergency room. In checking over Frank, the doctor
found his blood pressure dangerously high. He was immediately admitted to the hospital. For a reasonable length of time,
he was treated and medicated, but there was no response.

A surgeon was called into consultation. Because Frank's
blood pressure remained at such a high level, it was only a
matter of time before either a stroke or a heart attack would
end his life. Both the surgeon and the internist came up with
the same diagnosis—malignant hypertension. Both recommended the same treatment, a bilateral cervical sympathec-
tomy, the removal of the sympathetic ganglia on both sides of
the spinal column in the neck. The expectation for good results
was very low but the life expectancy in these cases, unless
something could be done, was only one to two years at best.

The damage to the eye grounds and the albumin in the urine already showed that profound damage had taken place.

The operation lowered the blood pressure only marginally. The time came for Frank's discharge from the hospital and he asked if I would follow his case. The medical records forwarded to me by the internist and the surgeon made it very clear it was only a matter of time before Frank would die. When I took his blood pressure on his first office visit and found it to be 250/135, saw the damage to the eye grounds, and his abnormal urinalysis, I reached the same conclusion. He was on the best anti-hypertensive medicine available in 1955. In spite of this, during the next three weeks, I saw Frank's blood pressure gradually creep upward. I felt helpless just standing by.

At that time, I had a Boy Scout Explorer Post, and some of the boys and their girl friends were meeting in our home every Monday night for prayer and Bible study. As was my custom when I had a difficult case of this kind, I would tell them, without giving the name or the condition of the patient, that I had a case that I needed for them to hold up in prayer so I would be led in what to do. About two days after their prayer meeting, the idea came into my mind to get Frank to a healing service. But at that time there were no healing services in Richmond. My Grandmother Ritchie had been an Episcopalian and I remembered that she had a prayer book I looked over several times after she died. I thought I remembered reading that they had prayers and anointing the head with oil and the laying on of hands for the sick.

At the time I was an Elder in the Presbyterian Church in my neighborhood. I knew we didn't have a healing service. In fact, when I had asked the minister about having one for my aunt who had the cancer, he looked at me like he thought I was either going off the deep end or trying to convert him to Christian Science. Thinking back about my aunt, however, reminded me of Mr. Rufus Womble, who had taken over as the minister for my aunt and had been so kind and gentle with her. I knew he was still in Richmond, still an Episcopal Priest and at the same church. I decided to give him a call.

When I called Mr. Womble, he was very friendly and definitely remembered me from my aunt's case. I explained to him the problem I now faced with Frank, and asked Mr. Womble if he would have a healing service with Frank at his church. He said he would but suggested it be a private service with just Frank, his wife, me and himself. He also requested that I not tell anyone about the service since he did not know how his vestry would react. To this I agreed and made arrangements to have Frank at the church two days later at eleven in the morning.

When the four of us met at Mr. Womble's church, doubting Thomas that I was, I took Frank's blood pressure just before we went down the isle to the altar rail and found it to be around 255 over 148. I didn't tell either Frank or his wife the results, but I was deeply concerned. Mr. Womble followed a very dignified service, praying over Frank with his hands on Frank's head and then making a cross as he anointed Frank's forehead with oil. As soon as it was over I asked Frank how he felt. He said a headache he had had all morning was gone.

Imagine this modern-day DOUBTING THOMAS' surprise when I led Frank back to the back pew and took his blood pressure again and found it to be 150/88. When I told the rest of them what had happened they were ecstatic.

I wasn't the one who told anyone in Mr. Womble's church. He 'let the cat out of the bag,' to someone in his church and this someone told the head of his vestry, who had a brother at Dr. Alfred Price's church in Philadelphia, Pa. The vestryman told his brother they had a minister who had gone crazy and had started having healing services in his church and was even claiming that a person had been healed. The brother, who was used to attending Dr. Price's healing services, told his brother that Mr. Womble wasn't crazy for following the orders of Jesus, for that was what all Christians were supposed to do; he [his brother] was, for not believing in the teachings of Jesus.[34] Later Mr. Womble, my wife and I went to Dr. Price's Order of St. Luke's Services at his church when they were having an International meeting of the Order, and all of us came back members of this order. Mr. Womble went on to hold the same position that Dr. Price held in the O.S.L. He also started an outstanding healing ministry in Little Rock, Arkansas, where he was sent by the bishop in 1958.

Frank's blood pressure remained in the high normal range during the entire time I followed him in Richmond, which lasted through June, 1964, when I left to move to Charlottesville, Virginia. I'm not sure, but believe he died from a heart attack in 1966.

Further Thoughts About Spiritual Healing

In all three of these cases, I feel that the part I played was to follow the orders of what I was being led to do. In the case of Mary Sue, both my wife and I had just returned from a spiritual retreat where our faith in, and expectations from, praying to God had been raised to an extremely high degree. My training as a physician mitigated against my believing that a severed spinal cord could be healed.

If one makes a study of Dr. Luke's gospel in the New Testament of the Bible, we see a physician, as one would expect, very interested in the healing ministry of Jesus. He researched and recorded 24 cases of healing miracles that Jesus performed. This is more than the other three Gospel writers recorded—and Dr. Luke also stresses the part that faith played in these healings.

Mary Bugg exhibited that kind of faith in this case more than anyone I have ever known, except Jesus in the case of Lazarus. My only part in this case was to be motivated out of my love and concern for two friends, a thing that any physician would have done.

The third case, Frank's, came as a result of my concern for my friend and patient, and my and the Reverend Rufus Womble's being willing to follow the dictates of the early church as recorded in James.[35]

What caused the Christian church to stop following the example set by its leader? I became enough interested in this question to begin some study and have read quite a few books on the subject. The shortest and best book I have come across is *The Great Physician,*[36] by Lindsey P. Pherigo. He brings out two very important reasons for this failure. The first reason is that Jesus patterned his life and teachings in the same belief system that the Old Testament prophets had before him. They believed God wanted health for His people. The order of the Jewish priesthood, on the other hand, believed God sent illness as a punishment for sins. Jesus, to me, seemed to teach that our sins, which we engage in through ignorance or voluntarily, brought sickness upon ourselves. He taught that things which proceed from the heart caused dis...ease, just as we have found in psychophysiological medicine today.

One of many other points Lindsey Pherigo,D.D. brings out[37] is the part that Basil the Great contributed to our idea that God sent illness upon us.

From this type of thing written in the fourth century until the *Malleus Maleficarum,*[38] published with the Pope's blessing in 1487, a person can see just how far the church had departed from the teachings and example of love and compassion of its leader, Jesus the Christ. This last book, along with organized religion from the fifteenth through the seventeenth century, caused the death of over 600,000 innocent women in the tragic witch hunts that it set loose in Europe, England and America. If any M.D. believed in this sort of so-called Christianity he would have to give up the practice of medicine and psychiatry because it would go against the will of God. Thank God, Jesus taught us that God's will was for health.

Finally, to answer the excuse that the church has too often given as the reason for not believing in spiritual healing or having healing services in the church: "What about all the people that are prayed for and don't recover? You'll hurt their faith." First let me bring forth something that most physicians, nurses, psychotherapist, ministers and priest who work with the ill have come to realize. There are some people who have too many secondary gains from remaining sick and unconsciously want to remain ill. God will not take back the free will that He gave us.

There are others who have been hypnotized by society and their religious beliefs into believing that a vengeful God wants them to remain ill. There are illnesses that lead unto death that are beyond our limited human ability to comprehend why. In this category are the elderly and possibly some young people whose work on this plane of existence is finished.

I see this decision as God's business and not ours. There are massive numbers whose death is caused by their own or somebody else's carelessness, certainly not God's. As a follower of Jesus, The Christ, and a physician, I feel our duty is to always ask for a loving God's will to be done in all prayers we make, where we are not sure of what His will might be in a case. Certainly with His knowing what the future holds, He is in a better position to determine what is best for our and His loved ones than we who are limited in our perceptions to this earthly plane. This I also believe: We never have the right to take away hope and love from anyone, and I can find *no example* from Jesus where He said to anyone who came truly seeking His help, "I am sorry, it is my Father's will for you to suffer, you miserable sinner."

Chapter 11

Understanding Two Different Sexual Orientations

The Iroquois Indians have a wonderful saying, "Don't judge your fellow Indian until you have walked in his moccasin for six moons." In the study of psychiatry we learn about projectionism, which translates into, "When you point at your brother, you have three fingers pointing back at you." Both of these sayings bring out a truth we all need to face. Judge not, that you be not judged.

Judging our fellow beings immediately builds a wall between us, and that wall increases the likelihood of misunderstanding. Misunderstanding leads to all kinds of difficulty in interpersonal relationships. Nowhere is this more evident in our society than when it comes to the lack of understanding we have about people who have different sexual attractions from ourselves. I hope that by sharing some of the things which I have learned from my research and studies into two of these conditions, you the reader will develop more compassion for the people who may appear so different from ourselves. The first condition is exhibitionism, or as known by its slang term, "streaking". The second is homosexuality. In both cases as in the rest of this book, I shall be looking at the etiology, or what causes such condition to develop.

Thomas Jefferson, the founder of the University of Virginia, is often quoted for some of the outstanding remarks that he made. One of these that impressed me was this one. "For here we are not afraid to follow truth wherever it may lead, nor to tolerate any error so long as reason is left free to combat it." This is so important to the University of Virginia and the atmosphere for learning at the University which Mr. Jefferson created, that it was inscribed on his statue located on the lawn of the University. This quotation, along with my psychiatric residency, compelled me into a greater search for finding the cause of a condition rather than just examining the results.

We can bring about real change only by removing the cause of a condition (if it lies within the realm of possibility), never by cussing its existence. Jesus said, "You shall know the truth, and the truth will set you free."[39]

Section A
Some Understanding of the Cause of Exhibitionism

When I was in my psychiatric residency, I had two cases of exhibitionism referred to me which involved the lives of two young men, both of whom had been in prison for exhibiting. I felt that I had an obligation to apply everything that I had learned and was learning to try to free them from this terrible compulsion.

Before going into psychiatry, like most laymen, I believed that boys and men who flashed or exhibited (exposing their male genitals) before females, (child, adult or both) did so intentionally and were dirty-minded. I quickly learned, as I began to study the problem that I was wrong on both counts. I learned this in connection not only with exhibition but with many other conditions. In psychiatry we use the term 'compulsion' a little differently from the way it is regularly used in English. It means an irresistible or uncontrollable impulse arising directly from the unconscious mind and therefore not subject to reasonable control.

My first case of exhibitionism was referred directly by a lawyer friend who had heard I used hypnosis in my medical practice even before I had changed to the practice of psychiatry. The lawyer called and asked if he could send a client to see me, with the idea that I would use hypnosis to help this young man who had started exhibiting when he was 17 years old.

When he came in for his psychiatric history and mental status I found a polite, personable, clean-minded 23 year old married man. He had already spent time in jail and regardless of this had had two more convictions in the past year. The judge had informed his lawyer that he would be facing a long jail term on this second conviction since it was quite evident he wouldn't control his exhibiting.

The lawyer had discovered the same thing I discovered in taking his past history. This man had been very reluctant to admit he had such a problem because he was so terribly

embarrassed by his behavior. Even more important, in listening to this young man the lawyer and I both began to comprehend something that the judge and most people didn't
understand: It wasn't that he wouldn't control his behavior;
he couldn't, even though he was facing another jail term.

As I began to research the literature on these cases, I found
that "Exhibitionists tend to fit into the average range of
intelligence. The occupations of exhibitionists are
predominantly skilled trades and laboring type of work, with
a preference for manly occupations. The exhibitionist is most
likely to exhibit right after puberty or just prior to marriage
or pregnancy or right afterwards."[40]

The more I studied in depth the background of these cases
the more typical I found my patient's case to be. These men
never show themselves to anyone but females. Putting them
in jail had no effect upon them, and, as with my patient, the
compulsion becomes worse right after marriage or the birth
of a child. What I found as I treated more and more of these
cases is that the tendency to expose themselves becomes worse
when they are under any kind of tension.

Again, my case, like most in the literature, had no conscious
understanding of why he exposed. As Sigmund Freud and
most psychoanalytic theory taught, it was caused by severe
unconscious castration fears.

After I explained to him that hypnosis, as we use it in
psychiatry, has no danger, I taught him how to relax so that
I could induce the hypnotic trance state. I took him back
through age regression to the worst thing that had ever
happened in his life. He centered upon an event where his
Mother was spanking him when he was three years of age. He
had urinated outside in the yard. His mother came rushing
out and, in anger, pulled his little shorts down, bent him over
her leg and hit him on his bottom. She also hit his penis and
testicles with her hand, which caused him a great deal of pain
and fright.

Before bringing him back to a conscious state, I gave him
two post-hypnotic suggestions: "When your mind is ready to
consciously remember what happened to you at three years
that made you afraid something had happened to your penis,
you will." I also gave him instructions tailored especially for
his case, which would assure him that he had a normal penis
and was a normal man. Following this first hypnotic session

he ceased to exhibit. He was given seven more hypnotic sessions, with all of the post hypnotic suggestions being more strongly enforced. Within three days after the first session, he had fully recalled the spanking incidence.

On the seventh and last session, while hypnotized, he was given the suggestion that a picture would form in his mind which would explain his tendency to exhibit. Upon coming out of the trance state he described a symbolic picture that formed in his mind and interpreted himself as a castration fear that had come about as a result of what happened when he was three years old.

When the judge learned that he had received psychiatric treatment for his condition, instead of sending him to jail, as he had threatened to do, he put him on two years' probation. My patient fulfilled his probation. Ten years later when my patient came through town and stopped by to see me, he still had never again exhibited.

I had eight more cases, with only one of them returning to showing themselves. A clinical psychologist, an instructor at the University of Virginia Hospital Mental Health Clinic at the same time as I when I was using my hypnotic technique, tried my method in nine cases and followed them for as much as three years. None returned to exhibiting.

When we begin to understand how much our superstition and ignorance can cost our fellow human beings, it is heart-breaking. Almost all of my adult exhibitionists have had to spend some time in jail before they were referred to me, and I can find no evidence where a true exhibitionist was ever cured by incarceration. The gossip and the way society has treated them is just as bad when you hear about what they have had to suffer through. We are better now and more educated, but we used to be as critical and as frightened of epilepsy and cancer. As a wonderfully kind minister friend of mine said to me, "The patient with AIDS today is suffering the same treatment that the patient with leprosy suffered in the Old Testament."

Section B
Some Understanding of the Cause of Homosexuality

During my travel with the Risen Christ through four realms of life after death, I was not shown anything in any realm that made me feel that He condemned the homosexual, any more than He condemned the heterosexual. What I was shown by Him was that He condemned sexual promiscuity in either sex because this was sex without love. In the realm that I considered to be Hell (because it was totally devoid of love and motivated by hate, revenge, bigotry and pure lust) sexual acts were being attempted and used to hurt and destroy the other being.

Too many Christian churches, which are supposed to have Jesus as their leader, certainly have not followed His example of love and compassion for the downtrodden in their actions of persecution against the homosexuals. Some of the leaders of the church have even tried to keep hidden the proper interpretation of The Story of Sodom And Gomorrah (Genesis 19:1-29),[41,42] and to persecute the priest and ministers who have tried to bring out the correct interpretation. I shall have more to say about this in my chapter about the part that organized religion has played in the cause of mental illness and human suffering. I bring this out because some church people's attitude caused more than five cases of homosexuals that I have done research on, or treated, to become agnostic. I would be afraid to hazard a guess as to how many suicides among homosexuals these attitudes have helped to bring about. These have been suicides caused by the attitude of people who have the audacity to call themselves Christians. I say 'audacity' because I believe that a true Christian is one who searches for truth, and would take the time to find out the cause of homosexuality.

In 1967 I won the William James research award given by The University of Virginia for my work and research into the causes of homosexuality. The paper is entitled: *Some Aspects of the Problem of the Etiology of Homosexuality*. What I am writing here is the result of that research and study as well as my looking further into the literature on the subject since then.

I do not believe we can say there is only one cause of homosexuality in either the male or the female, any more than we can say there is only one cause of cancer. Many top researchers have been working on this question. It seems, as in so many other cases, if we are going to understand the roots of homosexuality it is not a question of "either/or" but of multiple causes. My work and research drew me to the following observations and conclusions:

Before we can discuss anything we have to define it. Defining homosexuality is as difficult as defining heterosexuality. Although many authorities would prefer and use a much wider definition, in this chapter, I shall limit my definition of homosexuality to any type of sexual behavior by an individual with a person of the same sex which leads to a sexual orgasm.

The attitude toward homosexuality in the United States by the legal profession is best evaluated by Dr. Thomas Szasz.[43] He states in his review of the laws pertaining to homosexuality that a homosexual act between males, though not between females, is an offense in every state of the union. Dr. Szasz says, "For many years on both sides of the Atlantic jurists and physicians have in the main agreed that homosexual acts taking place in private between consenting adults should not be subject to criminal law. This view by American and English leaders in law and medicine has, however, so far not been reflected in medical legislation. As long as people seek through their legislators and by means of criminal law, to influence the private sexual conduct of adult members of society, it will be impossible to differentiate adequately between sexual acts that offend the public safety and welfare and those that do not." The overall view of both the legal and medical professions and of society as a whole is that it is a crime because it is unnatural.

Where have our ideas come from as regards homosexuality and its natural or unnaturalness, and the way we view it morally? Rattray Taylor says,[44] "In societies that conceive of their deities as mother-figures, incest is regarded as the overwhelming danger and is hedged with taboos, whereas homosexuality has little importance. Conversely, in societies that conceive of their deities as father-figures, homosexuality is regarded as the overwhelming danger and is surrounded with taboos and condemnation." He goes on to say that the Hebrews were originally a matrist society and had no taboos against homosexuality. Only *after* Moses and the ten commandments was any admonishment given against homosexuality. This came about as a warning against having sexual relations with the male prostitutes in the temples of non-Jewish gods for fear it would lead the men away from the worship of Jehovah.

It was only after the present interpretation of Genesis
19:5-21 that homosexuality began to suffer such condemnation from first the Jewish and then the Christian community.
I can find nothing in the four gospels where Jesus said anything about homosexuals.

What is psychiatry's view towards the etiology (cause) of
homosexuality? Sigmund Freud[45] felt that it was like being
born left-handed instead of right-handed, and he also thought
that all humans were born bisexual and went through a
homoerotic phase on the way to their gradual evolution into
heterosexuality.

Dr. Joseph Wolpe and many others of the behavioral school
believe that it is a learned phenomenon as a result of early
and persistent positive conditioning with objects of the same
sex. It seems to me that this view is strengthened by the
findings of Karpman,[46] who found that some previously
heterosexual men who engaged in homosexual practices while
in prison found it difficult if not impossible to return to normal
heterosexuality after release from prison. (The possible error
that I see in Dr. Karpman's work is whether or not he could
establish that these men weren't bisexual to start with.)

Dr. Denniston[47] states that bisexuality or ambisexuality is
a biological norm and feels that exclusive heterosexuality is
culturally imposed.

My own research[48] and the work of Bene[49] and Bieber[50]
all bring out the importance, as significant etiological factors
in homosexual cases, of the way the male child is rejected by
or unable to form a close relation with the father and has a
dominating or seductive mother.

At the time I did my work in the study of the effect of
chromosomes on homosexuality, the electronic microscope
was not developed enough to rule in or rule out the part that
gene and chromosome abnormalities played. In February,
1990, Dr. James Miller, head of research on chromosomes at
the University of Virginia (a man who was such a help to me
in my research on chromosomes when I was working on my
research project) told me that he felt reasonably sure that
there had still been no breakthroughs in the field of genetics
since I had done my research. He has quite a few research
papers on chromosomes to his credit and certainly keeps
abreast with the latest discoveries pertaining to conditions

thought to be caused by sex chromosomes or their abnormalities.

After I had written my research paper, Dr. Ian Stevenson[51], my teacher and friend, who along with Dr. Appleby inspired me to always keep searching for the truth, was kind enough to call to my attention two other possible causes of homosexuality. First, in his research in Southeast Asia he had come across a number of cases of Gender Dysphoria (individuals feeling that they should be the opposite sex), which is thought to be caused by a previous life in the opposite sex. A second possible cause: being raised by a single parent of the same sex and thus not having the opposite parent in the home to fall in love with at a very young age. Modern psychoanalytical thought teaches that the reason we develop into heterosexuals is that in mimicking the same-sexed parent, we fall in love with the opposite-sexed parent. This is where Freud's oedipal and electra complexes come from. I later had three cases in my practice where I felt having only the same-sexed parent in the home was definitely the cause of the homosexuality in the child. The two males had lost their mothers and the female had lost her father at the time of their birth or soon after and no substitute had been brought into replace them. They had all been raised by the same-sexed parent, and these parents were very kind and loving. It was very easy to understand how the child could grow to love their own sex when this was the first strong love object.

What can we conclude from our review of the literature, the most modern and up-to-date research and the work of many physicians, psychologists, anthropologists, sociologists, youth leaders and teachers? First of all, I believe that all of us would say that there is no simple answer as to the etiology of homosexuality and that there are multiple factors that bring it about. Of course we would have to say the same thing about heterosexuality.

Secondly, when we study all the books and reports about the incidence of homosexuality,[52, 53, 54] it seems we end up with a Bell Curve very similar to the Intelligence Quotient. At one end we have from 6-10% male- and 3-6% female-preferential homosexuals. There are as high as 20-35% bisexuals in the sense that they have had at least one or more homosexual experiences to the point of orgasm (included in this group are adolescents who engage in mutual masturba-

same sex). There are a very few ambisexuals, those who enjoy either sex equally. It is impossible to obtain the number of people who are latent homosexuals because of their unconscious denial of any homosexuality tendency, although their fear of homosexuality and their tendency to pick on and abuse homosexuals often gives them away. (These are also often the men who must brag about every women they have sex with, to keep proving to themselves that they are not homosexual.) Then come the majority of people who are heterosexuals: 55-65%. There is yet another group that some of us feel is out there but not enough research work has been done to determine the number who are exclusively psychologically heterosexual. This is the group that have no interest in their own sex and that you would never see in a sorority or fraternal organization. Lastly there are those people who are completely asexual. I know of no research or study that has been done on this group or how many would be in it.

What it seems we should conclude from this information is that humans cannot all be placed in one category when it comes to their sexual preference and behavior. Just because we fit into one slot does not give us the right socially or morally to say that those different from us are wrong or evil or outside of God's love. I do know from having read the four Gospels and having been conducted through four realms of life after death by The Risen Christ that he is far more critical of judgmental and unloving behavior than He is of any sexual relationships based on love.

III.

Searching For The Truth That Can Free Us To Live

Chapter 12

You've Got to Realize That You Are Dead

It is 6:30 a.m. Outside, it is light now. When I was awakened at 5 a.m., by what I believe to be the Holy Spirit, it was still dark. I feel God has just shown me, through nature, a great truth.

I awoke realizing that God had used my editor to let me know that this chapter had to be changed. I felt guided to get up and sit at a table, and for an hour and a half, I have been sitting here in a meditative state, listening deep within and looking out the sliding glass doors at the mouth of our creek, which enters into the Chesapeake Bay.

My editor had said that the first two sections of the manuscript were changing his life, but that Chapter 12 was losing him because it cursed the darkness rather than lighting a candle, and used too many generalities.

The first thought that came into my mind was to change the name of the chapter to its present name, "You've Got to Realize That You Are Dead".

Now, this shocked me and caused me to start thinking and really meditating. I remembered that God had said to Adam (in Genesis 2: 16 & 17) "for on the day that you eat from the tree of the knowledge of good and evil, you will certainly die". God couldn't have been talking about physical death because physically Adam lived to be 930 years old. So God meant another kind of death, spiritual death.

This becomes even more clear when we read Matthew 22:32, Mark 12:27 and Luke 20:38: "...God is not a God of the dead but of the living." Death, in the sense that I felt the Lord or Holy Spirit was putting in my mind, meant we have to realize that we are spiritually dead, i,e, separated from God.

Next He brought to my mind that fact that at 5:00 a.m. it had been completely dark outside, as physical death is at first. You couldn't see anything. But, as our planet turned towards the sun, making it appear that the sun was rising, what had been dark became flooded with light; the shadows of darkness were dispersed. So it is with our spiritual darkness when we turn towards the Son of God. He brought brilliant light when He came into my room, as I recorded in telling of my death experience.

The third thing He placed in my mind was that the great teachers of psychiatry and psychology have been correct in helping us to understand that we have learned a lot of things from the wrong source, which has brought about our spiritual darkness or death. As an example, misinformation and prejudices have been passed down to us by our parents, grandparents, teachers, ministers, physicians and all the early authority figures in our lives. Our newspapers, radio and television programs continually expose us to misplaced values. Most people of the past have been as dead to GOD as we are. Seeking knowledge from them as to what is right and wrong, and living by their sense of values, leads to our own spiritual death.

My meditation finished with these thoughts.

"You have gotten across some of the miracles that God had done to and through you in the first two parts of the manuscript. Now, if You will turn to Me as the earth has been turning toward the sun and becoming flooded with light, I will point out the major truths you have learned which have helped your patients and will also help the readers of your book."

"You can't give out something that you ain't got, no more than you kin come back from where you ain't been", the grand old black minister said. His English may have left a lot to be desired but his thought content was right on target.

The show "South Pacific,"[55] in its song, "Carefully Taught", has these profound lines:

"You're got to be taught to hate and fear.
You're got to be taught from year to year.
It's got to be drummed into your dear little ear.
You're got to be carefully taught . . .
You're got to be taught before it's too late,
before you're six or seven or eight,
to hate all the people that your relatives hate,
you've got to be carefully taught."

The above lines are referring to the negative things our

parents teach us. I'm not referring to the parents alone but to all the authority figures in our early life that I have mentioned.

This chapter will help the reader realize, from the things I have learned from my earlier experiences in youth work and psychiatry, the things which I believe help kill our soul. Like the rest of medicine, psychiatry is excellent in its knowledge of pathology, or what kills or destroys. It has not become as efficient, though it is certainly trying, in knowing what brings about good mental health, or life in the sense of which I'm writing.

First, as in any good mystery story, we have to discover that we have a murdered body. In our case this has been difficult to find because we haven't realized that it is us. We failed to realize that we were dead for the same reason that Adam and Eve failed to realize that they were dead. Evil made us think God was lying to us in order to keep something good away from us. "If you break God's command you won't die," says Satan to us both at the time of the Garden of Eden and now.

In the first part of this chapter I shall try to get across some of the things that helped to bring about our death. The next part centers on the truth that simply identifying the murderers and the weapons they use will not raise us from the dead any more than hanging the murderer in any murder story will restore the victim. It does call to our attention that some of the victims are coming to life and makes us ask the question, "How and why is this coming about?" It seems to me The Christ held some of the answers to this questioned when, as Jesus, he stated, "I am the way, the truth, and the Life,"[56] and, "if you have seen me you have seen the father. No one comes to the Father but through me." I believe that understanding what He meant when He said these things will bring us back to life and make us truly alive.

Pogo, in the funnies, expressed a great teaching of Jungian psychiatry when he said, "WE HAVE MET THE ENEMY AND HE IS US." Let us look at one of our first murderers, for he belongs to our own household, our parents and early authority figures. I shall use two examples:

One of the most common errors we make as parents today is being overindulgent. This has certainly helped lead to such things as crime and drug addiction because it teaches the child to expect instant satisfaction in life. Children who are continuously given toys, and have every need met even before they want them enough to ask for them, become bored and begin to expect parents or adults to do everything for them. Later in school they develop an inability to think and do things for themselves because they have grown accustomed to having someone always do things for them.

Because they have not learned to be either assertive or aggressive, they begin to fall behind their peers in their advancement and development of social and educational skills. Then they begin to feel inadequate, but they still want the instant satisfaction which they were carefully programmed by their parents to expect. Since they now expect their classmates and friends to entertain them and meet their needs the same way the parents did, they are not only boring to themselves but to their peers. When their peers grow tired of their passivity, and of having to always do something to entertain them instead of the friendship developing into a two-way street, they drop them. Since the kids have also been given an excessive amount of money, they are the perfect target for the drug pusher offers guaranteed instant satisfaction in either the bottled, pilled, smoked or needled form. Taking drugs also helps to overcome the feelings of loneliness and being left out because they are again a part of a group, especially if they can financially help support their friends in the same habit.

Years ago, I started a youth movement based on teaching the youth that love both of self and others requires discipline. Eddie, a 13-year-old, had come out of a home where he was spoiled and given material things; neither of his parents had time enough to take time out to train him because of their business and social life. His father came to see me, asking that I take Eddie into this youth movement, The Universal Youth Corps, because he had begun to get into trouble with the juvenile court and was having trouble in junior high school. I explained that this was a very disciplined youth corps and required that the parents back us in our rules and regulations. At the time he promised he would because the Juvenile judge had told the father, "If you can't control your son's behavior, the state can".

Because we had a rule that the kids had to study two hours each night or be on the honor role, the first thing that happened is that Eddie's grades began to come up. If the youngsters didn't abide by the rules they could miss some of the interesting trips where they had a chance to learn both land and water skiing, mountain climbing, caving and our spiritual retreats. For this reason most of the youngsters wanted to remain in the corps. They also had to earn the money to buy their own uniforms. Eddie continued to do fine and the older boys and leaders took time to see that Eddie stuck to a task instead of giving up when he bumped into a difficult assignment.

Time passed and Eddie finished his parole, and then his Dad began to complain that we were being too hard on Eddie. Finally the day came when his parents wanted him to go with them instead of attending an activity that the corps had been planning for over two months. Eddie himself wanted to go on the corps activity but his father said no and pulled Eddie out of the corps. (Eddie did not get into more trouble: Even his short time of a year and a half in the UYC had taught him how to achieve for himself so that he could develop self respect.)

Dr. Missildine,[57] Professor of Psychiatry at Ohio State University College of Medicine, wrote a book for his medical students and resident staff which I have recommended to my patients and friends who work with people in any field. It is a great aid in helping us to understand some of the personality traits which are formed in ourselves and others. He is particularly good in helping us to understand how so many personality disorders are formed. One of the traits which he says is most prevalent amongst parents in this country is over-coercion, where "the parent constantly directs and redirects the child's activities in an anxious, nagging and pushing way, leaving little or no opportunity for the child to initiate and pursue his or her own interest and activities." Dr. Missildine points out that whether the child goes into a command-resist cycle or becomes openly rebellious or goes into passive resistance depends on the age of the child when this over-coercive attitude of the parent begins.

Passive resistance, occurs when the actions of the parents start so early that the only course the child can follow is to comply and obey without question. Because we feel more comfortable with the known than the unknown, we will ultimately manipulate our friends, spouses, bosses, and business partners into playing the same role. As overindulgent parents cause passivity in the child, so do some over-coercive parents. All of us have not just one but many children of the past within us.

Active resistance, or rebellion, starts when the parent's over-coercion comes later in the child's life, after the child has developed his own thinking ability, and has begun to make his own plans. These kids grow up with the attitude that whatever anyone tells them, they are going to defy. If their living is dependent upon their carrying out orders, they do so with smoldering resentment and an attitude of open defiance. This, in turn, causes the same tendency in the spouses and authority figures that the over-coercive parent had, which is, "you are going to do what I want you to do." Thus this adult has a real stormy time of it. These are the kids who, the moment you tell them that you don't want them to smoke, drink alcoholic beverages, or get into drugs, do, just to defy you. Dr. Eric Erickson, the renowned psychologist of Harvard University, invented the term "Negative Identity," by which he meant painting a picture of what you don't want the child to do or become rather than painting a picture of what you do want. These kids jump to grab this kind of bait.

It is also the Command-Resist Cycle that I believe helps to develop what psychiatry and psychology call the Compulsive Personality Disorder. These people grow up with a tendency to procrastinate and daydream; they often suffer from chronic fatigue. The over-coercive parent is defeated by the child's saying, when told to do something, "In a minute."

Here is an example from a case I had. Ann was dragged in by her Mother with the following main complaint about her daughter: "I have to call Ann at least five times each morning before she will get out of bed. She is getting so that she acts this way about everything I tell her to do."

After getting as much background history as I could from the Mother, I sent her out so I could get Ann's viewpoint on the problem. Ann was an attractive, blue-eyed, blond-haired girl of eight years of age. I think I gained her confidence when I explained to her that what she told me would be kept confidential unless I needed to tell someone, to save a person's or my patient's life. Otherwise, I would have to have her permission to relate anything that she told me to her parents. The first question I asked her was, "Why does your mother have to call you five times each morning before you will get out of bed?"

She looked at me with those bright blue eyes and with a smile on her face asked, "Would you get out of bed the first time if you knew your mother was going to call you four more times?"

Here is your Command-Resist Cycle. The major trouble happens when the child becomes an adult. She takes the same nagging attitude with herself because this is the example which the parent set for her. The child within her still reacts the same way, only this time to her own commands. She ends up in procrastination, postponing decisions and chronically fatigued by the internal battle raging within.

If Ann also had a perfectionist father, who set unrealistically high goals or always berated his own achievements and kept driving himself, then Ann would also have a tendency to push on to higher and higher goals until the time came when she would be facing burn out (exhaustion). These tendencies might cause her to turn to drugs for a crutch.

The resolution of Ann's case came when I helped her to realize that it wasn't her mother she was defeating but herself by the pressure she put herself under. She was having to rush at the last minute to get to school on time. When she didn't, the embarrassment she caused herself with her peer group, she came to realize, she didn't want or need.

Most of us have heard that the battered child becomes the batterer. This is all too often true, but why?

Let's suppose you have been raised in a ghetto where your mother herself suffered from neglect from one parent and desertion by another. She had no good example to follow since there was never anyone close to her she could identify with or feel loved by. She had to fend for herself and learn from a hard cruel world. Mother had to work so she grew up feeling alone and separated from the rest of society.

Then one day there came into her life a friendly, impulsive, good looking 17-year-old male, your father-to-be. He became very attracted to your mother, who was a beautiful but extremely shy, thin girl.

When he tells her that she will be his girl and she can depend upon him, she really falls for him. His dad had always had to work hard because his wife, your paternal grandmother, was the queen of the neighborhood when he came along and he had always had to spoil her and give in to her wishes. Because your dad identified with his mother (he was told he looked like her and had her ways), he too grew up to be demanding and had temper tantrums whenever he didn't get his way. Your paternal grandfather tried to spank him one time and to correct him when he became sassy and talked back, but your grandmother said he was just a cute little child who would outgrow it and to leave him alone. She continued to spoil him by giving into him particularly as he grew older and stronger. He always melted your grandmother down on the rare occasions she refused his wishes. He would end up getting his way by saying, "You don't love me."

He pulled the same trick on your mother when they were going together. Between her loneliness and her fear of his desertion, she gave in and you began. Then both of your grandmothers decided your mother and dad should be married.

By this time your dad was 19 and your mother 18. Your dad, because he had dropped out of school when the classes grew hard, didn't have the education to get anything but a job working in the corner filling station. He began to drink a few beers with the boys and then your poor mother started bitching because they hardly had enough food for all three of you. The moment she crossed him, your dad, who was going to be the great protector of your mother, became the attacker. As you grew and made some demands of your own as a two-year-old and cried when they were not met, your dad began to smack you around. You began to feel that you were no good and were told that you were just like your mother, "who can't do anything right."

You were also getting angry because both parents kept blaming you for their having to stay together and dad was too big for you to hit back. Mother was always feeling sorry for herself and she didn't know how to clean the dump that everyone called home. Finally the time came for you to start to school, and since you too had either been beaten by dad or given in to by mother (so she would at least have you to love her), you expected the teachers at school to act the same way.

By the fourth grade, the teachers couldn't control your temper tantrums because you had grown accustomed to getting away with them at home. Dad was drinking more and more now, and mother didn't dare cross either of you but seemed to pull more and more into a shell. In the fifth grade, a fourth grader made you so angry that you hit him with a rock and then you sassed the principal and got yourself suspended for three days.

By your 13th birthday, you had developed the reputation for being such a tough kid that the ghetto strong guys had decided to take you into the gang even though you were younger than most of the guys. All you had to do was to pass the initiation requirements. These were to steal at least three pocketbooks from the women out on the streets and steal a stereo radio for your big gang brother who was sponsoring you into the gang. You got caught stealing a woman's pocketbook when she wouldn't let go and you stayed there long enough, hitting her, that she had time to recognize you. She and another woman who was walking up the street gave a good enough description of you so that it was only a matter of time until the police picked you up. You might have gotten off had it not been for your reputation in school for hitting that fourth grader and being suspended repeatedly, after that, for being impulsive and uncontrollable. Now you are headed for the boys' correctional school.

This background history I heard time and time again from the principal of the school at the boys' correctional school. He had been one of my assistant post advisors when I was running the Explorer Scout Post. As the principal told me, there had been no spiritual training in these homes. The only thing that most of these kids had a chance to learn about Jesus was how to use his name in cussing.

In all of these cases, who should be arrested? The kids, the parents, the grandparents, society or Adam and Eve? Will filling our prisons and jails with these kids, with drug addicts and alcoholics, change anything? Does pumping out money to build more jails and schools give the answers?

No, at best it only protects us from the ones that would injure and steal from society. Again, to cure a dis....ease we must discover and remove the causes, and as we shall learn in future reading and research into our crime and drug problems, the causes are multiple and not simple.

What then is the solution to perhaps the greatest problem which we are facing in America, our crime and drug problem along with our falling educational standards?

First we must come to face the truth about ourselves both as an individual and as a nation. We have not been put here, as I have told many of my patients, to be cared for or be entertained or just to have a good time. We are here for the developing of our souls, our minds and that part of us— whatever you may wish to call it—that is eternal. If we don't, we are in a process of regression instead of a process of progression.

We have evolved into a materialistic culture and the cost is profound. To keep up with the Joneses has all too often pulled both parents out of the home and left the children deserted in day-care centers where we don't even pay the teachers minimum wages. This is the same culture that will pay a top professional athlete or actor over a million dollars a year to keep us entertained but only the smallest possible wages to teachers who teach the most valuable possession we have, our children.

No one has driven home to us the point that the most important job we as human beings have, if we want the world to be a better place in which to live, is to love and train the generation we bring forth into this world. To create better people we have to have a better pattern, but we have, for the most part, ignored Him whom God sent as the ideal pattern of all times. I believe this to be so important that my last two chapters are dedicated to driving home this point.

One of the first things I always did when I started treating my patients was to discover what they believed or were willing to bet their life on. We base our life on our beliefs, not our intelligence. Who was their favorite family member, hero, movie star, author? Once I discovered this, it wasn't too long before I knew what I would find was their strengths and weaknesses.

If I asked what religion they belonged to (trying to find if they had any spiritual basis for their life) and they said atheist, then I would switch to see which political party they belonged. In the deepest sense of the word, there are no atheists. All of us believe in something or someone. Ultimately I had to help these people realize that they had broken the first commandment and had made that something or someone into their God. This was very often the case with parents with a child or vice versa.

One of the best ways to find out who is your God in life is to look back at your check stubs for the past three years and find out what or who you spend the most money on. I would have them do this, then take a look at where they spent most of their time.

Immediately behind this, and along the same line, was the question, 'did my patients have a sabbath day in their life which they made holy or complete?' Did they understand that, as Jesus pointed out, God created the sabbath for man and not man for the Sabbath? Sabbath means a day of peace and rest, also a day of RE...CREATION. If not, I was alerted to look for BURNOUT. Often times I found the ministers most guilty of robbing themselves of this very necessary day in their life. The question is quite obvious: Is a burned-out person dead or alive?

We are the first nation in recorded history in so far as I can determine to set up a Pediacracy, by which I mean A NATION RUN BY CHILDREN. I came along in the mid-'20s when the basic attitude was that "children should be seen but not heard". My grandfather's generation was well portrayed by the movie "Life With Father," which brought out the almost total patriarchy of my grandfather's generation. This caused a reaction formation or, in lay terms, a reverse trend, and was one of many things which aided in the formation of the Women's Liberation Movement. Another strong sociological factor was the two World Wars in which women were called upon to take over jobs and duties that had been limited to men before.

The natural tendency for Mothers to be more protective and play a passive role before their children. Into this vacuum of parental authority marched the omnipotent two-year-old child.

The rightful male role of the father is set out throughout the New Testament of the Christian Bible and particularly in the four Gospels. Jesus taught by precept and example that the ideal father is God and it is this example the male human should attempt to follow. This idea of a firm but loving father is particularly expressed in St. Luke's Gospel by the story of The Prodigal Son (chapter 15: 11-32). The son in this story is the symbol of the rebellious attitude which all humans display, for the tale of The Prodigal Son is also the cosmic story of each one of us. The father, representative of God, is loving, kind, forgiving; yes, but he doesn't indulge his son's rebellious attitude against what the father has stood for. He doesn't go after the son. He waits until the son realizes the mistakes he has made and has come back to the Father asking forgiveness, asking to be taken back into the home. Then the Father does so.

In the first realm of life after death, The Christ showed me what happens to a parent who makes the child the center of their life, for, as I related, even after her own death the Mother was following her son, trying to tell him what to do and how to live his life.

The writer of Ephesians gives sound advice[58] about the relationship between the husband and the wife and also the relationship between the father and the children. He says, "Wives, be subject to your husbands as to the Lord; for the man is the head of the woman, just as Christ also is head of the Church." Men read and love to quote this verse but they forget the verse that follows after: "Husbands, love your wives as Christ also loved the church and gave himself up for it..."

When no one in the home has the final authority on any issue and spouses vote in opposite directions instead of coming to an agreement, then the children can drive a mack truck right between the parents.

Let's just suppose that the grandparents had been taught by precept and example in all of these cases what Ephesians[59] says, "Children, obey your parents, for it is right that you should." "Honor your father and mother" is the first commandment with a promise attached, in the words: "that it may be well with you and that you may live a long life." I did not understand that fourth commandment until I was interning in the emergency room at the Medical College of Virginia and saw 22 DOAs (Dead on Arrival), come in and learned that 19 of them were under 25 years of age and were doing things that their parents told them not to do, which brought to themselves and their parents dishonor.

At this stage it might be wise to remember another scripture, "God is not mocked. What a man sows that shall he reap." I wonder, if the kids had had this "drummed into their dear little ears", whether there would be as many into drugs and being killed by drug dealers as there are today.

It has also occurred to me that fathers ought to read the

fourth verse of the same chapter of Ephesians: "You fathers, again, must not goad your children to resentment, but give them the instruction, and the correction, which belongs to a Christian upbringing." I came along in a day when neither the parents nor the teachers spared the rod or spoiled the child.

Sure, as small children we have to be instructed by and obey our parents for our own good. The fourth commandment says, however, "honor your parents". To my surprise, I can't find one out of 10 people who can tell me what it means to honor your parents. It means to live so as to reflect or bring glory upon our parents. It seems to me that in order do this we must first live so as to bring honor upon ourselves. Most people get honor and obey mixed up. If we don't know this difference, how can we expect our children to know?

In the first realm after death, The Christ let me see things that would help me to understand the reason for the first commandment and the first part of the great commandment[60] "Thou shall have no other Gods before me" and "Thou shall love the Lord thy God with all thine heart and soul and strength." This, He showed me, wasn't put in the Bible for God's benefit but for ours. Certainly a Being that is intelligent enough to create a universe knows the rebellious nature of human beings and understands that the moment you tell someone he (or she) has to love you, he doesn't.

Remember when The Christ showed me the other beings (who had been human) in the taverns and along the assembly lines? Remember the mother following her son? They had disregarded or misunderstood the reason for the first commandment.

The Christ was trying to help me become aware of a great truth: God is the only One worthy of our devotion because He alone has our best interest and the development of our souls first, in His heart. Becoming addicted to food, alcohol or drugs will eventually either kill us or bind us to earth. Businesses, homes, and all material things don't have the capacity to love and protect us. Water flows downhill and so does the duty to raise and protect our children flow from the parent to the youth. Even birds have enough sense not to try to follow and direct the lives of the fledglings after they are old and strong enough to leave their nest.

There is another law we should have learned from the teachings of Jesus but didn't. We didn't understand that His teachings weren't just a great philosophy: They are truths to guide us safely through our earthly incarnation and incarnations in all other realms until we develop into the souls of light and love He showed me in the highest realm, beings who were growing like Him in appearance. We forget that He pointed out our ultimate destiny when He said, "You must become whole (wrongly translated perfect), even as your Heavenly Father is whole."[61] Jesus gave us a law as important to our understanding and safety as the law of gravity when He said, *"No servant can be the slave of two masters; for either he will hate the first and love the second, or he will be devoted to the first and think nothing of the second. You can not serve God and Money."*[62] This is the law of triangles.

The law of triangles to me is one of the most important laws I have ever learned. It has two major parts to it. The most important part teaches us to picture a triangle where three people are each at an angle or corner of the triangle. It says there can be only one positive side and two negative ones. As an example, picture your wife, daughter and yourself. If you and your wife get into a very animated conversation, your daughter is going to feel left out. When she feels left out she is going to either try to get her mother into a conversation, at which time you will feel left out, or she will get you into a conversation, at which time your wife will feel left out.

When a side begins to become set positively between the father and daughter (making the bond is more positive between the father and the daughter than between the parents) we call that the Electra Conflict. The same is true for a positive bond between the mother and the son, instead of mother and father: We call it the Oedipal conflict. These play havoc in a family, just as surely as a positive bond between a spouse and an outside person or business or sport. If this were fully understood in human relations, we wouldn't have murders and suicides by the odd man (or woman) out.

The second part of this law is that we want the fight as far from us as possible. Going back to the original example: I don't want an open break with my daughter and certainly not with my wife. If there is going to be a break in relationships, let it be between my wife and daughter, or wife and son, or wife and business. The other two people in the triangle also want the break opposite, or as far away from them as possible. This is why it has been added to our wedding ceremony, "What God

(LOVE) has joined together let not man put asunder. That means *nothing else can be the third person or thing in the triangle except God, not a child, girl- or boyfriend, mistress, or material object.*

It would be hard to count the number of alcoholics I have treated whose underlying character disorder was a passive-dependent personality disorder (people whose major symptom is being too passive and letting people take advantage of them). When the spouse would get tied up in an oedipal or electra conflict, rather than stand and resist they would escape into the bottle. I have also seen the son or daughter in an oedipal or electra conflict do the same thing, especially when one of the parents had a tendency to drink to excess. These people need to learn to be assertive enough to say to their spouse, "You married me, not our child." These same parents need to explain to the children, when they begin to act omnipotent and think they can replace the parent, "This home belongs to my spouse and myself, not to you. You do not set the policy in this home. When you establish a home of your own, you can set the policy in your home, but not mine."

The Christ showed me a very important truth in every realm through which he conducted me: We reap what we sow, both good and bad. We need to get this across to our children and say to them, "You can pick any kick out of life you want; you cannot pick the kickback. You can pick any thrill you wish: You cannot pick the ill. Those penalties have been set by a Loving God who runs a very orderly universe and tries to teach each one of us by life, to think before we leap." I tried to get these ideas across to my patients and as a result those who really wanted to change seemed to be changing into some of the most loving and kind people I have known. As one patient said to me at the final therapy session: "Doctor, I feel alive for the first time in years."

Chapter 13

Organized Religion: Is It Following God?

Jerusalem

I stood among my valleys of the south,
And saw a flame of fire, even as a Wheel
Of fire surrounding all of heavens; it went
From west to east against the current of
Creation, and devour'd all things in its loud
Fury and thundering course round heaven and earth.
By it the Sun was roll'd into an orb,
By it the Moon faded into a globe,
Travelling through the night; for from its dire
And restless fury, Man himself shrunk up
Into a little root a fathom long.
And I asked a Watcher and a Holy One
Its Name? He answer'd, It is the Wheel of Religion.
I wept and said: Is this the law of Jesus,
This terrible devouring sword turning every way?
He answer'd: Jesus died because he strove
Against the current of this Wheel; it's Name
Is Caiphas, the dark Preacher of Death,
Of sin, of sorrow, and of punishment.
Opposing Nature, it is Natural Religion.
But Jesus is the bright Preacher of Life,
Creating Nature from this fiery Law
By self-denial and forgiveness of sin.
Go, therefore, cast out devils in Christ's name,
Heal thou the sick of spiritual disease,
Pity the evil, for thou art not sent
To smite with terror and with punishments
Those that are sick, like to the Pharisees,
Crucifying and encompassing sea and land,
For proselytes to tyranny and wrath.
But go to the Publicans and Harlots go,
Teach them True Happiness, but let no curse
Go forth out of thy mouth to blight their peace,

For Hell is open'd to Heaven; thine eye behold
The dungeon burst, and the Prisoners set free!

William Blake, the English poet, penned these lines years ago but how true still today. Blake with these lines put into poetry, the history of *some* of the organized Christian Church, Judaism, Islam and most of the worlds religions. The Saint's of all ages in every religion have had to fight against the stayed, set, inside group who fought tooth and claw, every new revelation of God and life least it might topple them from their power as did most of the ancient pharisees of Jesus' day.

We can see the modern pharisees as they appear on our television sets holding up the Bible and saying that the bible says such and such. It is the interpretation of the bible according to them and if you do not agree with their interpretation then you are going straight to hell. I am not referring to the honest hard working men like Dr. Billy Graham and Dr. Robert Schuller who have given their lives to Christ in loving service and concern for their fellow human beings.

Nor am I referring to the dedicated men and women of all the religions and denominations who have made honest misinterpretations of the scriptures, for I am sure that everyone who sincerely searches the scriptures makes mistakes in interpretation of them from time to time.

I *am* charging the ones who have taught a religion of fear and hate, the ones who divide people into 'we' and 'they', Catholics versus Protestants, Protestant versus Mormons, Christians versus Moslems, and prejudices in any form. Our world can be traveled in a day. My generation had trouble even accepting denominations that were different in the same religion. Our children are now in school, colleges and universities with other students who represent the religions of the world. The history of the human race teaches us that many wars have been started over differences in religious beliefs. We live with the knowledge that we now have weapons that can destroy the human race. We had better begin to realize that we all have separate realities.

The merits of these realities had best be judged by which reality causes us to be the most kind, considerate and loving to ourselves and others. We cannot be responsible for what others do and how they live their religion, but if we claim to be the followers of Jesus, The Christ, we had better stop preaching and living the Gospel according to Caiphas, as Blake points out, and start living and preaching the Gospel according to Jesus. As I brought out earlier, when I met the Risen Christ he wasn't impressed by what church I had joined, but asked me what I had done with my life to show Him. He was asking me if I had been kind and loving to those around me.

Like most psychiatrists, I have a great deal of animosity towards the pseudo-religion of people like Caiphas. I have never met any psychiatrists, even among my orthodox Jewish friends, who understood what Jesus taught and were against His teachings. Sociologists, psychiatrists, psychologists and ministers have estimated that from 55% to as much as 85% of mental illness stems not from genetic or biochemical factors but from erroneous teachings and/or misunderstanding of the doctrines of Judaism and Christianity. In the next few pages I shall attempt to help the reader understand from some of the history of the Christian Church why Blake wrote the poem "Jerusalem", and why I ask, "Is orthodox religion following God?"

Persecutions

Man has consistently tried to create God in his own image by projecting his thoughts on God, rather than submitting and letting God introject His thoughts into us. We are supposed to be created 'Imago Dei[63],'—in the image of God—but by projecting on Him we have tried to create Him in our image.

From the very beginning of the Christian Church there has been a tendency to follow some man rather than the Christ. Paul says, "Agree amongst yourselves, and avoid division; be firmly joined in unity of mind and thought."[64]

The founders of the early church weren't in their graves before the church split into the teachings of the early church fathers and the Christian Gnostics. This evolved into two camps. The "in" Church Fathers and the "out" Gnostics. This "in group" became the Holy Roman Catholic Church, which, led by some of its popes, cardinals and bishops, brought about one of the greatest bloodbaths in history, the Spanish Inquisition. The word Inquisition, according to the dictionary, means "A judicial system of the Roman Catholic Church for discovery, examination, and punishment of heretics, active in central and southern Europe from the 13th to the 19th centuries, succeeded by the Congregation of the Holy Office: also called Holy Office. . .the Spanish Inquisition, an independent court of the Roman Catholic Church founded in Spain in 1481, notorious for its severities under the inquisitor-general Torquemada."

This was a bloodbath carried out against some of the most sincere Christian people the world has ever known, who were known as the Catharists and the Albigenses. They were that force that stood against the corrupt practices of the Italian priesthood of the Roman Catholic Church of the 11th century. This is so typical of human nature: The people who are most corrupt blame their evil on someone else. This is why Dr. Carl Jung invented the term "Shadow" to denote that dark side of ourselves that we try to ignore by projecting on to others. Imagine calling Christianity a belief system that carries out the death sentence against anyone who doesn't believe the same way that you do.

Who gave either the Inquisition or its successor, The Holy Office, the right to judge their fellow human beings? Does not the scripture say, "PASS NO JUDGMENT, and you will not be judged? For as you judge others, so you will yourselves be judged, and whatever measure you deal out to others will be dealt back to you."[65] Not only has the Roman Catholic Church passed very cruel judgment on the people who didn't think the same way that they did or do, but so have we all.

Before we develop a holier-than-thou attitude against our Catholic brothers let's look at what the Church of England's attitude was against the Baptist church here in America when they were first getting started. Look at the attitude against the Methodist in the United States who split off from the Church of England. We all need to be ashamed of the way we treated our Mormon brothers and sisters when they began. It doesn't matter whether we talk about the Gnostics, Martin Luther, John Calvin, John Knox, Joseph Smith, or whom: Let every soul who would follow Jesus, The Christ, beware when he or she would attempt to dethrone the Caiphases of any entrenched religion or denomination lest they get themselves killed.

The terrible genocide that we so-called Christians committed against the Indians of North and South America should have taught the world a lesson, but no, we had to add the action of the Nazis in World War II, the Communist atrocities against their people in Russia, China, Southeast Asia and Africa, and now the actions of the Islamic Shiites in the Ukraine against the Armenians. I believe that most thinking people today have a revulsion against these atrocities—but what about some of our actions and teachings of the organized church that are still out of alignment with the teachings and actions of the Christ?

Reincarnation

In the 5th verse of the 4th chapter of Malachi is written, "Look, I will send you the prophet Elijah before the great and terrible day of the Lord comes." Matthew records that "When He came to the territory of Caesarea Philippi, Jesus asked his disciples, 'Who do men say that the Son of Man is?' They answered, 'Some say John the Baptist, others Jeremiah, or one of the prophets.' 'And you,' he asked, 'who do you say I am?' Simon Peter answered: 'You are the Messiah, the Son of the living God.'"

Now, to me this certainly indicates that people in that age believed that the Old Testament prophets could and did reincarnate. I have read nowhere in the teachings of Jesus where He said, "You shall not believe in reincarnation," or where Peter, James, John, or Paul make such statements. I do read where he says, "On their way down the mountain, Jesus enjoined them not to tell anyone of the vision until the Son of Man had been raised from the dead. The disciples put a question to him: 'Why then do our teachers say that Elijah must come first?' He replied, 'Yes, Elijah will come and set everything right. But I tell you that Elijah has already come, and they failed to recognize him, and worked their will upon him; and in the same way the Son of Man is to suffer at their hands.' Then the disciples understood that he meant John the Baptist." There are other references that point to the fact that reincarnation was accepted by people of Jesus' time.[66]

Many of the early church fathers believed in reincarnation well up through the time of Origen (185 A.D.-254 A.D.) and it wasn't until after 402 A.D. when Pope Theophilus crusaded against Origen, that the doctrine of reincarnation began to fall into disrepute by the church fathers. It was believed that an Anathema against Preexistence was passed in the Fifth Ecumenical council, also called the Second Council of Constantinople, in 553 A.D. but it was discovered about the middle of the tenth century that that conference had nothing to do with Origen or Origenism.[67] Today the organized church and particularly some of the fundamental television evangelist loudly preach that anyone who believes or teaches such doctrine is damned and going to hell. Yet I know of no minister who preaches this way who is as dedicated to helping others, or has spent a life time of study and research so that he might bring the greatest knowledge and understanding of problems that face us humans, as Ian Stevenson, M.D.

From the time that I first met Dr. Stevenson (when he first came to Richmond in 1962 to interview me on my own near-death experience) through the present, I have never known any man more intent on finding the truth in every field into which he searches. Nor have I met any man whose word is any stronger a bond than Dr. Stevenson's. His concern for his fellow humans and his desire to help them through research is an inspiration to all his colleagues and friends. And as a scientist, his work is beyond reproach.

Born October 31, 1918 in Montreal Canada, he studied medicine at McGill University in Montreal and graduated in 1943. He took his hospital training and residency in internal medicine at the Royal Victoria Hospital, Montreal, then, due to a severe respiratory infection, had to switch to St. Joseph's Hospital in Phoenix, Arizona. After further training at Tulane University and the New York Hospital, he joined the staff of Louisiana State University School Of Medicine in New Orleans. During these years he studied psycho-physiological medicine and also became a fully qualified psychoanalyst. He later wrote a booklet on medical history-taking and another on the psychiatric examination. The former went into a second edition and has remained in print for many years.

In 1957 he was asked to head the department of Psychiatry and Neurology at the University; he set up one of the best eclectic staffs in academic psychiatry, having such distinguished staff members as Dr. Wilfred Abse of the Washington Psychoanalytical Institute, Dr. John Buckman, of London, England, and Dr. Joseph Wolpe, who is world renowned for his work in the school of Behavior Therapy. He resigned this position in 1967 to become chairman of the new Division of

Parapsychology, now called the Division of Personality Studies, at the University of Virginia. He still holds this position, and in addition is Carlton Professor of Psychiatry at the University of Virginia. His published papers both in psychiatry and concerning evidence of reincarnation are numerous. I feel that it can be safely said that he is considered to be the top expert researcher into cases of reincarnation in the Western World.

In his outstanding paper, "The Explanatory Value of The Idea of Reincarnation", Dr. Stevenson gives us some idea of the strict high standards of research and the amount of research that he does on each case to find answers to such questions as Phobias and Philias (strong interests) of childhood, unexplained skills in early childhood, difficult parent-child relations, the question of childhood sexuality and confusion about gender identity. As he said this work has not been done to replace knowledge we already have on these subjects but to add to our body of knowledge, particularly in areas where our knowledge is so incomplete that we still don't have satisfactory answers.

Ministers, priest, rabbis, lawyers, teachers and all of the disciplines dealing with human problems and sufferings ought to read his book, *Twenty Cases Suggestive of Reincarnation*. Dr. Stevenson, with the help of his colleagues and assistants, has now assembled data on more than 1,600 cases of the reincarnation type. Yet there are still a lot of people in our churches and society who are not inhibited from speaking on any subject when they have no knowledge of the subject.

A wrathful God

Another area that concerns us in psychiatry and psychology is not just the murders that the organized church of the past caused through some of its endorsed books and documents such as the *Malleus Maleficarium*, which brought about the witch hunts and innocent deaths of over 600,000 women mentioned in a previous chapter, but the suicides that the organized church causes today. I have had three cases in my own practice of medicine in which I know the reason for the suicide was the patients' having been excommunicated by their church because they divorced and remarried. Again,

Jesus certainly never pointed to this as being the unpardonable sin or one that can't be forgiven.

Why did the organized church tie into the great love feast, THE LAST SUPPER, the story[68] of the Phoenician woman of Syria who said to Jesus, when He was testing her faith, "Even the dogs eat of the crumbs that fall from the table"? How many times have I had patient's use this very phrase taken from the "Holy Communion," "We are not worthy to come to thy table" and say, "we are not worthy to come to Christ"? Just as detrimental to the person is the attitude, which has been passed on by too many of our churches, that we are inferior fallen beings who exist only because a just and wrathful God hasn't decided to strike us down yet.

What about Genesis 1:26, that said we are made in the image of God, or the word Gospel, which means "Good News"? Good news is what Jesus taught in John 3:16-17, "God loved the world so much that He gave his only Son, that everyone who has faith in Him may not die but have eternal life. It was not to judge the world that God sent His Son into the world, but that through Him the world might be saved." I thought that to have faith in someone was to believe what he said and taught, and I have always believed that believing in Jesus doesn't just mean joining some church but living by His teachings of love.

That brings to mind another misunderstanding the pseudo-church has created. This is best expressed by letters I have received in which the writers state that if I join their Church, and live up to what seems to me some very narrow-minded scriptures that they have taken out of context, and say that I believe in Jesus Christ, I shall definitely go straight to heaven the moment I die. This is shear unexamined theology. To believe in Jesus is a very difficult process because it means I have to try to learn to give up my will and follow His teaching day by day. We have tried to make being a member of a church so simple and easy that, as one of my teen-age boys said to me, "Doc, until I joined your youth corps and dedicated myself to trying to follow Jesus, I thought it was far easier to be a member of the church than it was to be a member of my Boy Scout troop or the Tri-hi-y Club."

To me, pseudo-religion, or, as Blake calls it, the "Religion of Caiaphas," acts like religious ostriches who bury their heads in the sands of tradition because they fear anything new that will bring change. They create a church full of spiritual pygmies. This pseudo-religion creates a religion of fear, hopelessness, and lies against the teaching of Jesus. All this is a perfect prescription for escape into insanity, drug- and alcohol-abuse. It takes away the joy and true challenge that Jesus taught. Isn't it time that we take Jesus seriously? He said in John 4:23, "But the time approaches, indeed it is already here, when those who are real worshipers will worship the Father in spirit and in truth." We need to realize a truth Christ taught which someone placed in this little poem when he wrote:

"There is enough bad in the best of us
and enough good in the worst of us,
so that it should hardly behoove any of us
to talk about the rest of us."

To worship God in Spirit is to act in the spirit of Christ, LOVE. To worship God in truth means to be willing to search for truth in every field of life through which we are led.

Chapter 14

Who Is Our Leader?
Who Is Teaching Us?

We have talked about the part parents and religion have played in leading us into the major problems which we are facing today. Now let's look at what we have created by tolerating the political, psychological and sociological milieu we have brought into existence.

During World War II, we often had to move both parents out of the home. Dad was in the armed forces, out on the farm or in a vital defense industry. Mother was caught up filling in wherever she was needed. Parenting was left to whomever was still in the home or children were put into the newly emerging childcare centers.

A song of World War I asked, "How're you going to keep 'em down on the farm after they've seen Paree?" After World War II the question became, "How are you going to get both parents back in the home?" The increasing mobility of the American society meant that grandparents, great-aunts and -uncles were no longer in the home and couldn't take any part in the child-rearing process. The family became subservient to big corporations, which began to move young executives around through at least four to six different cities before they were settled in at their level of competency. It became such a fixed pattern in the Southeast that we could predict where our friends in Richmond, Virginia had come from (either Atlanta, Memphis or Charlotte) or were going to (Dallas-Fort Worth, Memphis or Baltimore). This took the young couples away from their families and the traditions which had formerly helped to establish their behavior patterns.

At the same time, in the fields of psychiatry, psychology, and sociology, WASP (white Anglo-Saxon Protestant) values began to be attacked by young college professors who weren't dry behind their ears when it came to a sophisticated understanding of the overall picture of life. Now, having spent over 40 years working with teen-age and college-age groups both through my profession and in youth work, I realize that the

WASP or the WMCC (White Middle Class Catholics) didn't have all the right answers—as I have brought out in previous chapters. Both groups attempted, however, to base their beliefs in God as they understood Him, and the Ten Commandments as they interpreted them.

As bad as some of the interpretations might have been, both WASP and WMCC teachings were far superior to the promiscuity which was being lived and taught by some of the richest families in this country, some of these very liberal teachers in our educational centers and some of the Hollywood movie stars. The students who went through our colleges and universities during these years from the end of World War II through the mid '60s and '70s are now parents, script writers, movie stars, doctors, lawyers, bankers, politicians and business leaders.

We would not be accepting our social milieu as it stands today, if we hadn't been completely brain-washed by the very forces I've spoken of in these chapters. Look at what this has led us into. The average father spends only 15 minutes a day with his children. Both parents, by the time they get home from the pressure of work and keeping up with the Joneses, are so tired or tied up in the social life of the community in which they live that they turn the baby-sitting over to Mother TV.

How qualified is Mother TV to take over this position of parenting? Over the last few years I have heard every standard of ethics and morality made fun of and derided in some substandard movie or talk show.

No wonder our teen-agers drive the way they do when they see their movie star heroes drive the way they do on television detective serials. Examine with me just one type of injury, the head injury that results from reckless driving, assault, and gun wounds. The following statistics were taken from an address given by John Perticone on March 2, 1990, to the International Association of Industrial Accidents Boards and Commissions:

Review of Financial Implications of Head Injuries
I. Acute Medical Care
A. Average length of stay: 60-90 days
B. Average cost per diem: $2,000
C. Total cost: $150,000

II. Acute Rehabilitation Costs
A. Average length of stay: 90-120 days
B. Average Cost per diem: $550-$600
C. Total cost: $60,375

III. Extended Rehabilitation
A. Average length of stay: 15 months
B. Average cost per month: $13,000
C. Total cost: $195,000

IV. Residential Program For Remainder of Life
(Average age of head-injured: 15-25 years)
A. Average length of stay: 30-60 Yrs.
B. Average Cost per annum: $60,000 - $125,000
C. Total cost (45 * $92,000): $4,162,500
D. Total lifetime average: $4,567,875

All of the above doesn't begin to be able to put a price-tag on the suffering and frustration to the patient and the family. Over-all, 87% are returned to some degree of independent living and 59% to some degree of employment.

No wonder a lot of our youth are seduced into trying drugs when they heard songs like "Puff The Magic Dragon" and were told by their older peers that this referred to smoking marijuana. Also when they learned their favorite singers like Elvis Presley and some of the Beatles were using Drugs. I can't find statistics that give what I believe is an accurate account of the number of youths who were using drugs in the late 1950's, or how many per 100,000 population are actually using them today on more than just a one-time basis, but our increase in crime and prisoners per 100,000 population does show us the tip of the iceberg because so many of the youth have to resort to crime to maintain their drug habit.

Some of our best "Who Done It" television mysteries have the heroes and heroines jump in bed with almost every new star who comes on the series. Now turn to the morning news shows: When the five minutes of today's news is over, our children watch these same stars glorified as the ultimate pinnacles of success.

If this isn't enough, when we get to the news itself, look at the behavior of too many of our top political and business leaders. Observe the farce of some of our television ministers who claim to be the last word from God. There are some of these preachers, because they now have a great television following, suddenly have gone into politics, deluding themselves, and trying to delude the public, into believing that they have the knowledge and experience necessary to run the country.

It is easy to criticize the great sports figures who have helped set the wrong example for our youth when it comes to sexual promiscuity and drugs, but let's look at my noble profession of medicine. The doctors themselves, by lack of self-control, are now helping to increase the number of drug addicts in this country. My own branch of medicine, psychiatry, that is supposed to have the answers to all the mental problems, is second only to dentists in suicides.

And what about some of the doctors, lawyers, insurance companies, and the takeover business leaders, who have pushed the cost of caring for the sick and the mentally ill in this country to where none of us can afford it anymore?

President John F. Kennedy said, "Ask not what your country can do for you, ask what you can do for your country." Who taught the people they could have privileges without taking on responsibilities?

What makes the American Civil Liberties Union think that we have to protect the individual who would tear down and destroy this great nation founded on the belief not only that God exists but that we should worship Him?

Who has let the doctrine of instant sexual satisfaction replace the belief and hope that we may find someone we love enough to give up our lives day by day to bring happiness into both sets of lives?

Who gave the right to stop teaching the true meaning of the word of adultery (having intercourse with someone you don't love) to our youth? No one has told me that God removed the seventh commandment or the cost of breaking it.

Teen-Agers are naturally group-oriented, and one of the great problems they fight with themselves is trying to fit in. By the time people move into their twenties, however, they are supposed to be moving out of group worship and trying to come to deal not with the question, "Do I fit in?" but "Do I stand out as the individual I was created to be?"

Of course, society is a group. We have our men's and women's clubs. But in them we are trying to be not all the same, but individuals working for a common good. The media would have us believe that we are "normal" when we act the way that most people act and that "normal" is the goal. We shall take a look at this dangerous concept in the next chapter when we ask ourselves the question "What is Man?" What we need to notice here is that when promiscuity and shooting drugs become normal, in an age when we are surrounded by AIDS, then we are playing with disaster and ultimate suicide.

Our youth need to be taught this hard, cold reality from the time they are five years of age. They need us to get honest with them and ourselves and admit to them that we keep bidding on contracts with them as parents, teachers and preachers that we can't keep. As an example: The parent who says to the youth "You can't go down lovers lane" is not only painting a negative picture of something he/she doesn't want, but bidding on a contract with his or her youngster that he/she can't keep. There is no way, in our mobile society, that a parent can keep up with every place a teen-age or college-age youth goes. What we do have is the obligation to teach them this: Yes, they can pick any thrill they want but the Creator of this world hasn't given their generation or ours the right to pick the ill—or change the cost of the bill that comes with the thrill.

These are some of the bills:[69]

1. Statistics on AIDS:
At present, 121,645 diagnosed cases.
One million have the virus.
Deaths so far: at least 72,580
Present trends projected through 1992:
365,000 cumulative diagnosed cases
363,000 cumulative deaths
Incidence in 1992 alone if trend continues: 80,000 cases, 65,000 deaths.
Number of people that will be living with AIDS: 172,000, requiring treatment at a cost of $5-13 billion.

The trouble with all of these statistics is that the AIDS cases are only the tip of the iceberg. They don't tell us how many HIV cases we have. These are cases that have actually been infected with the AIDS virus but are asymptomatic. A patient can carry the disease and not show it sometimes for as much as eight to ten years. In December, 1989, there were 118,158 cases of AIDS. Among children, 5% had received it from blood transfusions for hemophilia; 81% had been infected by their mothers during their formation and 2% of the 81% caught the disease from nursing the mother. The most tragic rise in the statistics is the growing rate of infection among the adolescent population.[70]

When we look at the headlines, we see still greater cost and tragedy. Just one example, this headline from the January 23, 1990 Richmond (Va.) *Times-Dispatch:* "Study shows 14 youth cost state $2 million." The article cited a study by a court psychologist showing that 14 young men age 13 to 19 had been charged with 685 offenses. They all came from single-parent families, had IQs in the average to above-average range, and had committed their first crime at age 13. The psychologist said, "It would be speculative, but not exorbitant, to suggest that this population of youth, a mere fragment of the entire juvenile population in the city of Richmond, has probably already cost in the neighborhood of five million to six million dollars."

The report said that the cost for 14 youth, studied in greater detail, was $2,038,409. This total did *not* include the actual cost for things such as the youth's welfare or food stamps, the cost of their crime over the years and many other services. What's worse, of the youths surveyed, 77% were still detained, and about 1/3 were in the adult correctional system.

The study concluded that, when paroled, most of them "would drift in a purposeless, aimless fashion seeking immediate gratification on a day-to-day basis, being highly vulnerable to increased criminal involvement."

The report didn't leave me with the impression that the incarceration helped at all. Crime statistics continue to rise each year. How we are going to be able to continue to pay for treating the results when we aren't doing anything to remove the cause?

2. *The Statistical Abstract of the United States for 1989 reported the following:*[71]

1. Prisoners/100,000 population

1950	1960	1970	1980	1984	1985	1986+	1987
110	128	98	135	185	200	215	230

In 1987, violent crimes rates were 68% higher for males

than females, also higher for theft. The younger persons, ages 12-24 had the highest victimization rates for crimes of violence and theft.

2. Homicides/100,000 population

	White Male	White Female	Black Male	Black Female
1970	6.8	2.1	67.6	13.3
1980	10.9	3.2	66.6	13.5
1986	8.6	3.0	55.0	12.1

Suicides:

	White Male	White Female	Black Male	Black Female
1970	18.0	7.1	8.0	2.6
1980	19.9	5.8	10.3	2.2
1986	22.3	5.9	11.1	2.3

The report in the National Crime Journal-115524, June 1989, gave the following statistics:

In 1964 the total of all crimes in the U.S. was 3,260,000. By 1983 it had increased to 37,001,200, an *eleven-fold* increase.

In 1964 the total of all crimes of violence was 240,000. By 1983 it had increased to 5,903,440, a *25-fold* increase.

All of the above statements and statistics raise the question of who is leading us and influencing our lives, but even more important is the question, "What are we going to do about it?" Spending money to try to reduce crime and our drug intake doesn't work unless we have come to understand the causes and remove them. This dis...ease is a spiritual cancerous growth within our society. Since society, in a democracy, is controlled by the people, and the people by their thoughts, then we need to re-examine our thoughts and the people and things which we let influence them. Certainly it doesn't sound like we are living what we have stamped on our coins, "IN GOD WE TRUST."

Carl Jung in his psychiatry speaks about our shadow, and Jesus said, "Why are you concerned about the splinter in your brother's eye when you have a plank in your own?" We had all better look at who and what is infecting our minds and souls.

We can not look at the cost of just one type of accident, head injuries, without asking the question, "Can we afford the accidents that we have in this country and not look more deeply into the cause?" When we look at the increase of crime and violence in our country and see a definite correlation between this and the amount of drugs we are consuming, then the question must arise: "After whom are our youth patterning their lives?" Certainly not after the men and women that the great middle-class WASP and WMCC of a generation ago looked up to.

It seems to me that we have forgotten the words of the song from the musical South Pacific: We must be carefully taught. We have forgotten the profound knowledge of the old black minister: "You can't give out something you ain't got, no more than you can come back from where you ain't been."

Our youth are being taught but by whom? There have always been some older children and teenagers waiting around the corner to pass on forbidden teachings and cuss words, but there were also the grandparents, aunts and uncles, the scout master, sunday school and school teacher who took the time out with us and spent time getting and keeping our interest in more wholesome things.

Children and young people are going to learn from somebody close at hand. With black and white ghetto children, where the single parent is herself all too often an immature adult or teenager, knowing nothing about training and discipline, it is no wonder that the neighborhood hoodlum and the television become the real teachers of the children.

It seems to me that television and the news media have enough tragic human-interest stories to use to get across to the hoodlums, drug dealers and all who profiteer from selling drugs the hard lesson of life: You can pick your thrills; life itself picks the ills that follow. You can pick the kicks, but life sends the kickbacks to those who ignore God's laws—kickbacks that can end not only in death but in far more severe suffering and penalties in the realms after death.

Chapter 15

What Is Man?

Who am I?

Where did I come from?

Why am I here on this Earth at this particular time?

These are three of the four questions most of us find ourselves asking sometime during our lives. The answers we might get to the questions largely depend on whom we talk to, the anthropologist, the evolutionist, the psychologist or the theologian. Fortunately or unfortunately (depending upon who you are and how you look at it), none of these disciplines has played much part in our concept of ourselves in the last two generations. Rather, we have let what comes across on television and in the movies set the ideals as to what is man.

For example a few years ago, a Gallop Poll showed that the following people were the most looked up to and admired by our teen-age and college-age youth:

1. Clint Eastwood
2. Eddie Murphy
3. Ronald Reagan
4. Jane Fonda
5. Sally Fields
6. Steven Spielberg
7. Pope John Paul II
8. Mother Theresa
9. Michael Jackson
10. Tina Turner

Either an anthropological or evolutionist point of view would, I feel sure, say that this proves our point, that man is in transition; man is an evolving creature.

Psychology and psychiatry aren't much better. They try to measure man against one of several models: the Cultural model, the Normal model, the Productive Model, the Self model, the Ideal model. Let us take a look at the strong and weak points of each model.

The Cultural Model: The cultural model declares that normalcy is based upon what the greatest number of people approve of as a role model. To me this is exactly what we are seeing; what our present day culture pushes as most popular. But suppose the culture is in a state of regression, instead of progression. Or suppose the models are engaging in very dangerous behavior to themselves or others? We saw what could happen when we had the Nazi or Stalinist Culture. Is the drug culture any less deadly?

The Normal Model: This states that the ideal is based on what is normal behavior, or, like our I.Q. Tests, where the majority fall. To me this would remove any possibility of progression from the human race. It raises the same perception that our normal teen-ager raises: Do we all fit in? If this is the model, do we have the chance to develop our God-given individuality?

The Productive Model: The emphasis here is on functioning in a healthy productive way. Are they happy and productive in what they have picked as a way of life? The trouble here is that as I become very productive and efficient in one department of my life, I'm more than liable to do so at the expense of another department. I might become a very efficient company man and totally fail as a family man. This borders on the perfectionist personality disorder which leaves us blind to the area of our personality and life which become inhibited at the expense of our perfectionism.

Otto Rank, who was a disciple of Freud and did much study into the development of the human personality states that there are three types of men:

1. The Creative man, who is able to shape his own environment to serve his needs.

2. The normal man, who adjusts to the environment as he finds it.

3. The Neurotic man, who is in between. He can neither shape his environment nor adjust to it.

Rank pointed out one of the difficulties with this. If society itself is neurotic, then the most normal man trying to adjust to it will become neurotic. This seems to be exactly the case with the pressures which we let most of our business, families, churches and clubs bring upon us.

The Self Model: The self model uses our own judgment as the standard of comparison. A few years ago Frank Sinatra made a song popular entitled, "I Did It My Way." I Think the Quakers put their fingers on the trouble with the Self Model when they said, "Everyone is queer, save thee and me; and sometimes I think thee a bit queer too."

The Ideal Model: This is picking a man or woman from the past or present whom we feel is the ideal person, or comes closest to fitting our concepts of what the ideal person should be. But this is still another form of the subjective or the Self Model of man. It is based on the community's concept and again fails in an attempt to define exactly what the ideal is. Some of the Caesars weren't the first and will not be the last to declare themselves the ultimate ideal of what we should become. The danger here is that the next stage to ripe is rotten.

The Perfect Model[72] "Be ye therefore perfect, even as your Father which is in heaven is perfect."[73]

"Good Master, what must I do to win eternal life? Jesus said to him, 'Why do you call me good? No one is good except God alone.'" Therefore, the first thing we can say about perfect is that it doesn't mean good either in the Bible or in the dictionary. The dictionary gives these definitions:

"1. Having all the elements or qualities requisite or necessary to its nature or kind; complete.... 4. Accurately or closely reproducing or corresponding to a type or original; exact: a perfect replica."[74]

Therefore we can say that a perfect man is a complete or a whole being and is a perfect replica of the original model that God was referring to when He said, "Let us make man in our image and likeness..."[75] So God created man (male and female) in His image. Now we are told in most denominations of the Christian religion that no one has seen God, but we have seen the One God was referring to when He said to the One with Him from the beginning, His Son, let us create man in Our Image.

From here we can say then the complete replica or whole man should have the following attributes:

He is a *creative thinking being* and because he is, he uses his creativity. This is the very type of man that Otto Rank referred to as the creative type, who shapes the environment to fit his needs. Everything that I can think of that God created in man is neutral. God left it to man to decide how he was going to use his faculties. But the whole man, as we have seen in the Christ, uses his attributes to express love and to accept it. Therefore in all the department of his life, he is governed by love for himself and others. I put it this way because we really can't see others as lovable until we see ourselves as lovable.

When it comes to sexual activity, the complete man is governed by love for the partner, unlike most mammals (who are motivated by the procreative instinct) or too many "average" men (motivated by the sexual urge). This means he or she doesn't have sex just because it feels good or because everyone else is jumping into bed, but because he or she uses it as the highest physical expression of love. He doesn't whisper sweet things in the partner's ear so that she will whisper nice things back in his ear. He doesn't use a kiss as an upstairs persuasion for a downstairs invasion of the partner. He doesn't say to the partner, "You don't love me if you won't go to bed with me." This type of behavior is narcissistic love of the self, not thinking of what might be best for the partner. Since love carries with it respect for the beloved and discipline of self, the relationship must be between two people who have come to first know, respect and admire each other. They are not going to procreate unless they love each other—and the offspring who comes from that sexual act—enough to care for him or her.

This leads right into the next important attribute of the whole person, a *sense of responsibility*. The best way I know to describe this is to understand and apply the meaning of the word responsibility, i.e. responding or using one's ability to meet the challenges of life. To do this we have to be aware of both our abilities and our liabilities, our assets and our defects, and act accordingly.

The whole being must, as the name implies, be able to integrate the different departments of his life:

The Intellectual Department
This may be thought of as that department which governs our research and study. The learning and desire to learn is continuous without his developing either conceit or a closed

mind. His interest should have many facets and there should be a strong desire to pass on to others the good and beneficial things that he has learned. This may mean a great deal of time spent in formal academic study and education, but I have met many people who have never had the chance for much formal schooling but are very smart intellectually because they have trained themselves to observe and learn from other people and from what they see around them. Certainly the whole person can transpose what he has learned in one area of his life to other areas and times where it is appropriate.

The Moral Department

This covers such things as the integrity of the person as related to his honor, honesty, principles, loyalty, scruples, respectability and sensitivity to fair play. None of us would want to have to live with a moral prude, but neither would we want to have to spend time with people who are debased, dishonest, disloyal, or deceptive. A whole person has all of the positive moral attributes without flaunting them.

The Financial Department

Too often we tend to gauge a man's financial success in terms of dollars and cents. Our whole man must have a much more integrated view of finance than this. He must be able to stand on his own financial feet, but finances can't master his soul. He owns the material things but they don't own and enslave him. He is not stingy; but generous—up to the point that it doesn't damage him or others. (He doesn't use his financial wealth to buy or control others; he doesn't give gifts which he can't afford because of his feelings of inadequacy.)

The Physical Department

Is he built like Mr. Universe? Does he have to win the title of Mr. America? No, but he does respect his physical body and tries to take care of it because he realizes that it is a gift from his Creator and the Creator cohabits it with him. He learns the laws pertaining to health and gets the proper amount of rest, recreation, and food. He takes the time to have adequate physical and dental examinations and doesn't push himself or let anyone else push him to the point of burnout. He is productive without stress and attempts to find and remove the cause of stress when he encounters it. He does not blame others for his failures, i.e. he doesn't use projectionism or denial as an ego-defense mechanism.

The Social Department
This covers the breadth and quality of his interpersonal relationships with his family, his business associates, his friends and his enemies. It is in this department that the whole man differs to the greatest degree from the average man. As Pogo said long ago, "We have met the enemy and he is us". This is exactly what Carl Jung stressed in his psychology when he called our unacceptable side our "shadow". It was this part of our ego, Sigmund Freud said, that uses the defense mechanism of denial and projectionism to pass our faults to others instead of recognizing them as our own.

As we use the terms in psychiatry, "denial" means refusing to admit having character traits in us which are unacceptable to our concept of ourselves. "Projectionism" means projecting the fault off on to someone else. The typical example of this is the latent or unconsciously driven homosexual, who has to act like a Don Juan and keep bad-mouthing homosexuals because it helps him to deny consciously his own unconscious homosexual tendencies by projecting them and hating them in the homosexual.

This is exactly the same thing Jesus was saying to us when He said, "Why do you look at the speck of sawdust in your brother's eye, with never a thought for the great plank in your own eye?" The Whole Man or Woman doesn't do this; and, ceasing to do this, he or she isn't as judgmental. Ceasing to be judgmental, they are more loving of themselves and their fellow humans.

In 1960, I watched Dr. Frank Laubach, founder of the Laubach Literacy program, call his friend U.S. Senator Hubert Humphrey, to ask him to start a Peace Corps.[76] He demonstrated another attribute of the whole man in his social department: an international concept of family.

Dr. Laubach was on the advisory board of the Universal Youth Corps of Virginia which I had started and occasionally came as a speaker to address the teen-age and college-age youth. He often asked, "How big is your family? Is it only as big as yourself? Your family? Your community? Your state? Your country? Or the world?" Then he would hold up a globe of the entire world. His family was the downtrodden, poor and uneducated people of the entire world. He loved them enough to create ninety-eight different written languages, and then teach these people how to read and write their own language. We desperately need men and women who have a national and international concept of family today, as we see communism and it's control falling in Eastern Europe, especially in the Balkans. These nations, newly freed from communism, are being kept from forming strong democracies by ethnic pride and prejudices arising and destroying their sense of unity.

The Perfect or Whole Man must have a *sense of humor* and be able to laugh at himself and not take himself or others too seriously when they act temporarily insane with negativism. Sure, we live in a world which is full of negativity and faults, but it takes a good sense of humor to overcome these and be able to visualize a better world.

The Whole Man should have a *sense of destiny* to his or her life. By destiny, I don't mean that genetics, astrology, environment or the position of his birth in a family is the thing which he allows to set his destiny. All of these forces *impel* us to a more or less degree, but none *compel* us, because our creator has given us free will. To have a sense of destiny, he needs to research his past enough to form some concept from whence he came, and needs the capacity to learn from his past mistakes which history shows him. Equally important, he must have a sense as to where he wishes to head.

In this, there must be a *sense of timing*. As a youth leader and physician, I have seen myself and others make serious mistakes by planning too far ahead and also by not planning far ahead enough. Circumstances in life can change very suddenly and unexpectedly; therefore, one also needs to retain *flexibility* in his timing and in his planning. The Whole Man needs to do this in relation to himself and to others.

Finally the Whole Man needs to develop the AGAPE type of love. If he has developed all the other qualities and has not developed this, then as Paul says, "I am none the better."

How to obtain and maintain this type of love is the great secret. There have been hundreds of books and articles written about this type of love, AGAPE, and all the attributes which it demonstrates. The greatest living example I have ever seen was the One I met in my near-death experience at Camp Barkeley, the Risen Christ.

It would be good if just being in His presence could and

would create this in man. If it could, then all of Jesus' disciples would have immediately been like Him and acted as He did, and so would I. We know this wasn't the case with them, nor has it been with me or others who have had the near-death experience and met Him. We are led to believe, however, that the disciples grew to have this type of love in them. It seemed to have taken a lifetime of living and learning from Him, first with Him on the outside and then with Him on the inside, to accomplish this. Most of us don't do this because we let some priest, minister or rabbi tell us how to live and what God and the Risen Christ are like instead of taking the time to come to know God personally through prayer and meditation. This is what our *Perfect Model* should and can do and be.

"What is man that thou shouldst remember him,
mortal man that thou shouldst care for him?
Yet thou hast made him little less than a God,
Crowning him with glory and honour."[77]

Yes, created with God as a father and Christ as brother, we are just a little less than God, but, as the 82nd Psalm says, when we don't learn to act and live as the Gods he created us to be and fulfill our destiny, then we shall die as men.

Chapter 16

Our Ultimate Destiny

Is it accidental that I and others had these near-death experiences? Or did we die, or come close to dying, or face a cataclysmic experience in our lives, because a great and loving God was trying not only to save us but to bring us back in order to tell and show in our living, a better way of life for our world?

Yes, as the great apostle Paul wrote, we have to be careful whom we contact and consult with over there on the other side of death, for there are some very mixed-up beings, and beings who have gone astray and would lead us astray if we listen to them. This is not the case, however, if we have met the Risen Christ or the numerous beings who are working with Him who are trying to help make this world a better place.

Even in this world we say in our courts that ignorance of the law is no excuse. How much more is this true in God's universe and in nature on this planet. It is my belief that a loving God does not send catastrophe upon us; we bring it upon ourselves because we won't listen to Him, to His Son, or to the prophets and great leaders of all times that He has sent trying to guide us. If you and I are one of these messengers who have been given a chance to meet Him or one of His beings of love and light He as sent to us, and we remain silent when we see the people in our world creating a "diverse" instead of a universe, then we are guilty of not doing our part.

Yes, it cost Jesus and the prophets their lives when they spoke out against the wrong practices of the organized religion and corrupt governments of their times. It has always been hard to stand for the difficult right against the easy wrong. Our Father, GOD, showed us that there is an ultimate destiny for all who would surrender to His will and leadership, as Jesus did. Even physical death couldn't stop this destiny, which leads to a realm where there exists truth, love, and life on a level that we can't comprehend until we have seen it.

Because of all the reasons stated previously, I have been living with this stupendous sense of destiny and the realization that I was given orders to return to this realm not because I had any desire to, but because I have a commission to pass on what I have seen and learned. My writing this book, particularly this last chapter, is an attempt to help show a way to reach the highest realm, heaven—not when we die but while we are alive. That is, I am trying to show how to become truly alive in any realm in which we live.

If there is one law just as certain in life as the law of change, it is the law that nothing stands still and survives. If I'm simply treading water when I'm out swimming in a river and do not swim toward one shore or the other, it is a certain fact I shall drown. The same law that governs these results also governs the fact that I'm either fresh and growing, or I'm wasting away from some disease and/or aging process, and am dying. Any businessman will certify to this reality: His business is either expanding and growing or it's shrinking and going out of existence.

Man has a destiny, an extremely high challenging one. When I say man I am speaking of something far greater than just the physical being, I am referring also to the part which we call spirit, soul, psyche or mind. There are those doctors of medicine (psychiatrists and neurologists) and psychologists who would lead you to believe that the mind and the brain are the same thing. I am aware that ever since 1650 A.D. we in the medical fields have been arguing the mind-brain problem and that numerically the number of doctors are about the same on both sides.

I can say, however, that I have never talked to anyone who has had a *near-death experience* similar to mine who wasn't as convinced as I that the brain and the mind are two different things. Like me, they believe that the brain has the same relation to the mind that a television set has to television waves. Just because one cuts off the television set doesn't mean the waves cease to exist. Just because the brain and body die doesn't mean the soul or psyche ceases to exist.

The ultimate form of man, whatever you may wish to call him or her, has a destiny to fulfill in God's universe just as surely as physical man has played his or her part in this physical realm. As we go through the different stages of life, either we are moving closer to fulfilling this destiny or we are growing further from it. If we are moving away from our God-created destiny, then in the deepest meaning of the word death we shall die, for one of the meanings of the word death as used both in the Old and New Testaments is that state in which one is separated from God.

To understand our ending we have to have some understanding of our beginning. So let's go back to the six-day or six-eon time when God said, as recorded in Genesis, "Let us create man in our image." That makes us also creators because God is a Creator. "Meister Eckhart explains what it means to be an image: "An image receives its being immediately from that of which it is an image. It has one being with it and it is the same being. We, who are the creator's image, share one being with the creator. Like God, we need to create."[78] Meister Eckhart also said, "The Soul among all creatures is generative like God is."

Now, man is created with this creative power but the Genesis account further states that after man had demanded his right to know both good and evil and was hiding from God, God called to man and said to him, "Where are you?" The 10th & 11th verses have man answering and saying, "I was afraid because I was naked, and I hid my self." God answered, "Who told you that you were naked?" The word naked would have better been translated into English as "inadequate." I interpret this, as a follower of Christ and as a trained psychiatrist, to mean two things. First I still see our Creator asking us, "Man, where are you in your relationship to Me?" Secondly, I hear our God questioning our source of information when we respond and claim we are inadequate or naked.

As Carl G. Jung brings out in his book *Man and His Symbols,*[79] the snake has always been a symbol. "Commonly linked with transcendence, because it was traditionally a creature of the underworld . . . and thus was a 'mediator' between one way of life and another." So I hear God still asking man where is he in relation to Himself, i.e., is he accepting just the instincts and urges of his physical ego or self, or is he in communion with God through his higher spiritual self, and the Holy Spirit within himself? Man has to believe something before he can act upon it. Our thoughts or beliefs create emotions. Emotions create feelings. Feelings are the things that govern our actions, not our intelligence or truths. If we believe a lie is true, we are going to act and react on or to it. Since we are creative beings, then our beliefs in lies create further lies and further separation from God since God is truth.

We apparently demanded the privilege of incarnating into the animal body and becoming subject to its strong physical urges and lower nature before we developed the responsibility for being able to handle this knowledge or had developed our higher spiritual nature. We see young and old people making this same mistake every day: people thinking they are mature enough to handle drugs, complicated finances and other things beyond their capacity. God still raises the same question when we hide from Him, our real source of truth and love: "Where are you?" On this plane of existence that we call Earth, we have wandered into a jungle that operates on the law of the survival of the fittest. Without Him to lead us through it, we are lost.

Religion separated from the leadership of God confirms our own negative thinking by telling us we are naked, or inadequate, and fallen sinners. It leads us into complacency by leading us to believe that if we join a church and say we believe in Jesus and that He died for our sins, we are saved. This is not what Jesus, The Risen Christ showed me, either when I was with Him or since I have returned to this life.

Certainly, Jesus and His Father, our God, knew if He came down here to Earth's plane and confronted us with the truth about our individual thinking and how far we had strayed from God's desires and teachings, we would kill Him. In this sense, as well as the more orthodox which the organized church teaches, I believe that He died for our sins. It is my belief, both from living in this life and from seeing the realms which He showed me existed in life after death, that He incarnated to teach and show us what man could become when reunited with Our Older Brother and our Father.

Unlike the false religions which too often preach a negative identity while serving the Holy Communion (by saying that we are dogs not fit to come to Jesus' table to celebrate the love feast with Him), Jesus came teaching good news. Quoting Psalms 82: 6, He asked, "Is it not written in your law, I said, you are Gods?" And did he not teach us to pray *Our Father* and tell us that He was our older brother? If God is our Father and Jesus is our brother, then we also have to be gods and not lowly worms. St. Irenaeus stated that God became a human being in order that human beings might become God. I would chance what he said only to the degree that I would say that Jesus showed us the God that GOD, OUR FATHER created us to be.

Even here on earth, the psychologists and psychiatrists have warned about creating a negative identity. One can't read the writings of Eric Erickson, of Harvard University, in such books as *Young Man Luther*, without becoming immediately aware of the dangers of creating a negative identity in a child or person. They have clearly taught the wisdom which comes from realizing that if we teach a person that he is a dunce, he will act like one. They also teach us that if we paint pictures of what we don't want in a child's mind, instead of what we do, what we don't want comes into existence in the child's or adolescent's life.

In two of the three temptations that Satan used on Jesus, he tried to create doubt in Jesus' mind about His being the Son of God, and the devil in various forms certainly tries to create doubt in our own mind about our true relationship to God. But Jesus doesn't. Jesus comes with good news, restoring our identity and saying, "The spirit of the Lord is upon me because he has anointed me; he has sent me to announce good news to the poor, to proclaim release for prisoners and recovery of sight for the blind; to let the broken victims go free, to proclaim the year of the Lord's favor."[80]

Jesus quoted from Isaiah 61: 1 & 2, which is saying the same thing as the message in the 82nd Psalm, what we should all do if we wish to fulfill our destiny as gods and not die as men.

We have wonderful promises found in Psalms 23, 27, 34, 91, and 121, and also from prophets like Isaiah, but we don't see and hear the full extent of the love and forgiveness God has for man until Jesus comes on the scene. As marvelous and magnanimous as both the love and forgiveness of God are, there is still something greater that Jesus brought us, which leads and directs us towards our ultimate destiny; the development of our souls until we have reached what He promised us when He said, "In truth, in very truth I tell you, he who has faith in me will do what I am doing; and he will do greater things still because I am going to the Father. Indeed anything you ask in my name I will do, so that the Father may be glorified in the Son. If you ask anything in my name I will do it. If you love me you will obey my commands; and I will ask the Father, and he will give you another to be your Advocate, who will be with you forever...the Spirit of truth."

The above quotations from Jesus raise two profound questions:

1. What does it mean to ask something in Jesus' name.
2. What does it mean to obey His commands?

If we understood what it meant at the time Jesus was living to ask something in a person's name, then I think we could understand what he would mean or say today.

From what I learned from being with the Christ, to ask something in His name means to have the same thoughts, feelings and desires that He has. All four gospels quote Jesus as saying that He surrendered His will to his Father. He said in the 14th chapter of John's Gospel that if we had seen Him, we had seen the Father. In Him, we saw incarnation of love the world has ever known. The second shortest sentence in the Bible (after "He wept.") is, "God is love."

It is time that the clergy and seminaries get honest with us and admit that any part of the Bible that disagrees with Jesus and His teachings of what God is like is wrong. The writings in the Old and New Testaments were passed through men of a certain day and age. The times in which we live, and our surrounding beliefs and circumstances, affect our thinking and distort our understanding of the truth just as surely as they affected and distorted the ability to perceive the truth of the men and women of the past. If we do not stop teaching the infallibility and inerrancy of the scriptures and popes and bishops, we are going to continue to lose to the secular world those intelligent men and women, who are truly seeking. Yes, we and they believe in the divine inspiration of the written scriptures in the Old and New Testaments—but we also believe that the only thing that is infallible and inerrant is that which proceeds out of the mouth of God: the Father, Son and Holy Ghost.

If infallibility means that the Old and New Testaments are correct in showing how far off all men and all women of all ages have been in understanding His will and Nature (except Jesus, who came from God and had perfect union with God), then I believe the Bible to be inerrant. If it means that everything the men and women of the Old Testament said and thought is to be taken as accurate and as literally as the teachings of Jesus about God, then I don't believe in the infallibility of the Bible.

I believe the Old Testament is wrong when it paints a picture of a God who approves of the murder and plunder of war, and wrong when it states that a woman is the property of a man, as stated in the 10th commandment.

I believe the Old Testament is wrong when it leaves the impression that it is wrong to place the male sperm cells any where but in a woman so that there would be more children to fight a war for Israel. I believe it goes against the will of a loving God to ever bring a child into this world when one doesn't love that child enough to try to do everything that is right and proper in order to take care of that child. The Bible teaches that even a sparrow doesn't fall from the air that God doesn't take note of it. How much more is a loving Father God going to want us to care for any children that we produce? How can any denomination, race or political government advise and encourage people to have children when they know that the parents are neither emotionally or financially prepared to do so?

I believe that both testaments are wrong when they say that a woman shouldn't be allowed to speak or preach in a synagogue or a church. This is the thinking of a very patriarchal male society that has projected its ideas onto God. I find that the Jesus of the four Gospels, and the risen Christ of my Barkeley, Texas, experience held both man and woman to be equally the children of God. I also noticed that He didn't act as though the color of a person's skin or creed made any difference to Him. What did make a difference to Him was whether we loved one another the way He showed us that we should.

What kind of omnipotent self-righteousness are we engaging in when we as men and women have advanced enough to recognize the evils of slavery and then say that we think the Bible is the infallible word of God when it gives permission for the institution of slavery? Certainly Jesus used the examples of the servant and master relationship in many of his parables, because He was speaking to the people who lived in times of slavery. He used these examples to point out to us that if human masters expected their servant and slaves to obey, how much more did a loving Father have the right to expect His sons and daughters to obey.

Our liberal teachers are right when they accuse us of treating the patient with AIDS today the same way that the people of the Old and New Testament treated the people who had leprosy. We act just like them when we condemn homosexuality when we don't even know the cause, just as we accused the leper of being punished by God until we found out in this century that it was a chronic communicable disease caused by a microorganism known as the Microbacterium Leprae. I'm not saying that homosexuality is caused by a microbacterium: I am saying that the causes are probably multiple and we don't understand all the causes, as I pointed out in chapter eleven.

But many religious liberals are wrong and just as guilty in some of their teachings, for there are those who would have us believe that if we can't scientifically explain something in the Bible it shouldn't be believed. Some liberals teach that the miracles can be explained away, and that the guidance of the Holy Spirit doesn't cause miracles to take place today. God's ways are beyond man's comprehension, and anyone trying to explain away the miracles is attempting to reduce God to their limited understanding of life.

Jesus, himself, tells us what it means to obey His commandments when He said, "A new commandment I give unto you: love one another; as I have loved you, so you are to love one another. If there is this love among you, then all will know that you are my disciples."[82] To be someone's disciple is to be trained by them. This is especially so in Jesus' case, for without Him in us training us through His Holy Spirit, I found out that neither I or any other man or woman could even love ourselves much less another human being the way that He loves us. As a woman once said to me, I have to first learn to love myself before I have any goodies to pass around to others.

This is our destiny that He prayed for in the Garden of Gethsemane: "But it is not for my disciples alone that I pray, but for those also who through their words put their faith in me; may they all be one: as thou, Father art in me, and I in thee, so also may they be in us, that the world may believe that thou didst send me. The glory which thou gavest me I have given to them, that they may be one, as we are one; I in them and thou in me, may they be perfectly one. Then the world will learn that thou didst send me, that thou didst love them as thou didst me."[83]

When we put our faith in Him, we will take the time to know and be with Him until we surrender our will to His control. To have faith in a person, we have to come to know him. We can read all about Jesus in the four Gospels. We can read all about His being in us as He said He would in the 14th, 15th and 17th chapters of John's Gospel. *We will never come to know Him any more than we know anyone else by just reading about Him.*

After reading about Starr Daily in his book *Release*, I had to meet him. By spending time and talking with him, I came to know him. The more time we spent together, the better friends we became and the better we knew and understood each other. To get to know the Christ we must do the same thing, but there is this major difference in the physical location between going to meet another human and going to meet the Christ. To meet Starr Daily I had to find out where he was located, which usually involved traveling quite a few miles. In Jesus' case, He said He is living inside of you and me and speaks through the Holy spirit which God has placed in us. Therefore my traveling to meet Him is learning to turn deep within and learning to listen when I want to communicate with Him.

Jesus said He would send the Spirit of Truth to guide us into all the truth.

About 30 years ago, speaking to about 3,000 teen-agers in Hershey, Pennsylvania, telling them about my experience of meeting the risen Christ, I explained that they didn't have to wait until they died to meet the Christ because He was inside them, and was more anxious to talk with them than they were to talk with Him. After the talk, I gave them the chance to write down questions for me to answer. The question most asked was, "How do I know whether it is my thinking or The Holy Spirit's or Jesus' putting the thought into my mind?"

I could only pass on to them what has worked for me. I told them I had made up four questions to answer for myself the same question which they were asking. If, when I asked these four questions, I received no answer, then I often found the Lord would answer the question through somebody else, or I would have to wait to see which doors He would open or close in my life to show me the answer.

I said that my test consisted of **L J T R:**

Is what is coming into my thinking **loving?**

Is it the type of thing that **Jesus** would say if He was standing in front of me?

Is it **truth** as far as I can comprehend?

Does it pass the test of **reality** of all ages? For God is the same principle of reality for all time.

I pointed out that the Holy Spirit speaking for the Christ never tells us the truth about ourselves without first making sure that we know He loves us. Evil causes us to tell the truth about someone else or about ourselves without love, and this can destroy us. Certainly God is truth, but He is always love, and uses His knowledge of the truth in a loving way.

To know whether Jesus would have said something, we have to become familiar enough with the four Gospels so that we know and can recognize His personality.

When He speaks to us, what He says may be hard to follow, because He is also life, which teaches us not just to live but to learn things that will cause us to mature and grow spiritually. He is always loving but sometimes it is a hard, disciplinary love. If we follow his orders there will come peace, joy, hope and happiness for He still teaches us the way to ultimate happiness. If what is coming into our minds is negative and pessimistic, then we can be sure that it is not from Him.

Across the ages, as He did in the Garden of Eden, God still calls out to man, "WHERE ARE YOU, ADAM?" Man, with the help of the dogmas of Western Christianity, has lost his way, and sees himself totally separated from God because Western Christianity through the Roman Catholic Church stressed *fallen* man, with Jesus dying for our sins on the cross. The churches have not explained our potential as gods, with our God-given creative power, and how necessary it is for us to be under the guidance of the Holy Spirit of God when we use this power.

Instead they lead us to believe that the church was given the authority to decide who was going to heaven, and that those who didn't join their particular denomination were going to hell. This is incongruous with the teachings of Jesus, The Christ, who told us the tale of the prodigal son not only to help us understand the love and forgiveness of God but to help us understand that the Prodigal Son is the cosmic tale of each and every human being. We have all forgotten that we are sons and daughters of the most high God; that our spiritual side, the soul of man, needs to return and have total fellowship with the Father. To do this we have to come to ourselves and realize that in this human plane of existence, our human, selfish side has led us down the road of materialism and of living only for ourselves, which caused us to turn away from our Father and our divine destiny and forget who we are. It caused our spiritual death.

Jesus went on the cross to show us that we must die to this human egotistical side in order to let the soul of man, which has carried the knowledge of who it is and from whence it came, come to life and into control.

This is our Ultimate Destiny, to reach out and begin to communicate with The Christ, so that He can lead us back to being alive: i.e. into that perfect union with our Father, and let Him pass His love and thinking through us to one another. We must come to know the living resurrected Christ within us, and depend on passing his love to one another and to God, because our human love isn't enough. When we recognize this truth, then, like the Prodigal Son Jesus told about, we will have "come to ourself"; that is, we will come alive, and will decide to go home, for we will know that even being a servant in Our Father's household is better than being dead spiritually, the way we have been living. Then, with The Christ, The Holy Spirit and our Father—all of us joined together—we shall be helping to create a universe and no longer a diverse.

This is what I believe Jesus meant when He said, "And I shall draw all men to myself, When I am lifted up from the Earth."[84] Christ showed us that He had to go through the death of His physical self in order for the resurrection of his spiritual self to take place. I think that his death on the cross *also* symbolizes that we must realize we are dead before we can be raised up by the resurrected Christ within us. I find it hard to believe that in our present state of spiritual death we can conquer our self-centered lower physical nature without going through the death and surrender of our will as did Jesus on the cross. I can say from the Risen Christ's having conducted me through four realms of life after death, that in the highest realm, He showed me beings who had followed his teachings and were now resurrected into spiritual beings who were like Him when it came to the love, light and life they put forth.

I believe Jesus did not incarnate *just to die for our sins,* but that he also lived and died to show all of humanity, regardless of race, creed, or color, how much God our Father loved us. He expects us to do the same thing. When we come to realize this, then He will truly be lifted up for we shall be keeping the great commandment, "love the Lord your God with all your heart, with all your soul, with all your mind and with all your strength. Love your neighbor as yourself."[85]

Our destiny is to not only come to know and rise above our human side, but, by following His example of dying to self, to come to know and activate, or bring to life, our spiritual side, which he showed was in every man, woman, and child. He showed us how to die to self and how to rise from the dead and ascend into our higher self, life.

I'm not convinced that all of the animal and human sacrifices that we as a race have made through out recorded history have ever removed sin. If sacrifice does that, it still is beyond my grasp. The dead can't raise the dead. A man in debt can't pay his own way out of debt, much less someone else's. Only a sinless Christ could do this.

What I do believe is that following the examples Christ set, from His birth through his baptism, transfiguration, and crucifixion—which required the surrender of His will unto God, even if it caused the death of all his human self-protective instincts—does remove sin, if we consider sin being anything that goes against the will of God.

I'm not saying that we have to make a sacrificial death on a cross as Jesus did. I am saying that we have to reach the place where we are willing to face the death of our self-centered nature so that our higher spiritual nature can gain control. I believe that being willing to follow such a total surrender to God's will will bring about a resurrection and ascension of the transformed self, which can change a world into a heaven on earth. He started this transformation first in Himself to show what can happen to all who would follow Him. It changed Him and all who followed Him because He surrendered his will to God our Father, who, He showed, is pure LOVE. Our destiny is to do the same thing in order to survive and change our world. His commission wasn't just to teach and show us how to reach the highest realm, heaven, but rather how to create heaven on earth.

Notes

Chapter 4
1. The New English Bible, Matt. 22:38, Mark 12:30
2. 1st Corinthians, 13:2

Chapter 5
3. Chosen Books, Fleming H. Revell Co.
4. John 14:6
5. Proverbs 23:7
6. A type of railroad boxcar made famous in World War I, designed to carry 40 men or 8 horses.
7. Frenchmen who worked with the Nazi occupiers in World War II.
8. The same as an emergency ward of a regular hospital.

Chapter 6
9. In *Through the Valley of the River Kwai.*
10. Acts 9:3-16

Chapter 7
11. "Make no mistake about this: God is not fooled; a man reaps what he sows." Gal. 6:7
12. Author, speaker, president of the Koinoia Foundation of Baltimore, Md., and Spiritual Life Leader of the United Methodist Church in Eastern Virginia.
13. *Release,* by Starr Daily, Harper & Brothers.
14. Author, founder of the CFO Camps of America.
15. John 14:9
16. Darell W. Amundsen and Gary B. Ferngren, in Marty and Vaux, page 65.
17. Late 4th-century Roman Church Leader Basil the Great's tract "Why Christians Suffer."
18. Lindsay P. Pherigo, *The Great Physician,* published by the Women's Division, General Board of Global Ministries, The United Methodist Church, pp. 13 and 14.
19. John 14: 9-11

Chapter 8
20. The American Heritage Dictionary, Second College Edition.
21. Ibid.

22. 1 John 4:19-21

Chapter 9

23. *Alcoholics Anonymous,* Bill Wilson, Cornwall Press, April, 1939. 1951 edition.
24. *Alcoholics Anonymous,* 1951 edition, page 369.
25. Women's Christian Temperance Union, a group of women who helped lead the fight for prohibition.
26. John 14: 20 and 14: 23

Chapter 10

27. Founder of the Christian Science religion. See *The History of Psychiatry,* by Franz G. Alexander and Sheldon T. Selesnick (Harper & Row, New York), p. 131.
28. Author of *Man, The Unknown,* Harper & Row, 1935.
29. Ambrose A. Worrall with Olga N. Worrall, *The Gift of Healing,* Harper & Row, 1965.
30. Glenn Clark, Ph.D., educator, football coach and author of many books, including *The Soul's Sincere Desire* and *A Man's Reach.* 31. Matt. 19 and 20.
32. Acts 12: 1-17.
33. Luke 7: 1-10, Matt. 8: 1-10
34. Matt. 10: 8, Luke 10:9
35. James 5: 14 & 15
36. Lindsey P. Pherigo, *The Great Physician,* published by the Education and Cultivation Division, General Board of Global Ministries, The United Methodist Church, 1983.
37. Pherigo, pp 13-14
38. Franz G. Alexander, M.D., and Sheldon T. Selesnick, M.D., *The History of Psychiatry,* Harper & Row, 1966, pp 67-68.

Chapter 11

39. John 8: 32
40. "The Use of Hypnosis in a Case of Exhibitionism," by George G. Ritchie, M.D., in *Psychotherapy: Theory, Research and Practice,* Vol. 5, #1, Winter, 1968.
41. *Reflections on the Gay Life,* by Edward W. Bauman. "The Bible and Homosexuality," pp 3-7.
42. *Living in Sin,* by John Shelby Spong, Harper & Row, 1988, pp. 136-142.

43. Thomas S. Szasz, "Legal and Moral Aspects of Homosexuality," in *The Sexual Inversion*, Judd Marmor, Ed., Basic Books, 1965, pp. 124-132.
44. G.R. Taylor, "Historical and Mythological Aspects of Homosexuality," in *The Sexual Inversion*.
45. Sigmund Freud, "Letter to an American Mother," American Journal of Psychiatry, 107: 746-787, 1951.
46. B. Karpman, "Sex Life in Prison," Journal of Crime & Criminal Law, 38: 475-486, 6/26/48.
47. R.H. Denniston, "Ambisexuality in Animals," *The Sexual Inversion*.
48. George G. Ritchie, Jr., "Some Aspects of the Problem of the Etiology of Homosexuality," University of Virginia, Department of Psychiatry.
49. Eva Bene, "On the Genesis of Male Homosexuality: An Attempt at Clarifying the Role of the Parents," in the British Journal of Psychiatry, 11: 803-811, 1965.
50. I. Bieber, etc., *Homosexuality*, Basic Books, 1962.
51. Carlson Professor of Psychiatry, former Chairman of the Department of Psychiatry and Neurology of the University of Virginia, author of more than 20 articles and of *Twenty Cases Suggestive of Reincarnation*, University Press of Virginia, Charlottesvile, Va.
52. W. Churchill, *Homosexual Behavior Among Males: A Cross-Cultural and Cross-Species Investigation*, Hawthorn Books, 1967.
53. A.C. Kinsey, et al: *Sexual Behavior in the Human Male*. W.B. Saunders Company, 1948, and *Sexual Behavior in the Human Female*, 1953.
54. W.H. Masters, V.E. Johnson, *Homosexuality in Perspective*, Little, Brown & Company, 1979.

Chapter 12

55. Richard Rodgers & Oscar Hammerstein, "South Pacific."
56. John 14: 6-21
57. W. Hugh Missildine, M.D., *Your Inner Child of the Past*, Simon & Schuster.
58. Ephesians 5: 22-25, Ephesians 6: 1-4
59. Ephesians 6: 1-4
60. Deut. 6: 5, Matt. 22: 37, Mark 12: 30, Luke 10:27
61. Matt. 5: 48
62. Matt. 6: 24, Luke 16: 13

Chapter 13
63. Genesis 1: 26
64. 1 Corinthians 1: 10-13
65. Matt. 7: 1-2
66. Matt 11:7, 10-11, 14-15, Mark 6: 14-16, Luke 9: 7-9
67. Joseph Head and S.L. Cranston, *Reincarnation,* Julian Press/Crown Publishers, pp 160-164.
68. Matt. 15: 21-28 and Mark 7: 25-30

Chapter 14
69. U.S. Public Health Service, Department of Health and Human Services, as of March, 1990.
70. Lisa Kaplowitz, M.D., "AIDS-1990," lecture given at the Medical College of Virginia Alumni Association Continuing Education Program, held April 7, 1990 in Richmond, Va.
71. U.S. Department of Commerce, Bureau of the Census, Superintendent of Documents, "Statistical Abstracts of the United States, 1989," 109th edition.

Chapter 15
72. Matt. 5: 48
73. Matt. 19: 16-17, Mark 10: 17-18, Luke 18: 18-19
74. The Reader's Digest Great Encyclopedic Dictionary, 1966.
75. Genesis 1: 26
76. After U. S. Senator John F. Kennedy won the presidential nomination, Senator Humphrey passed along to him Dr. Laubach's Peace Corps idea. After winning the election, President Kennedy turned over the idea to his brother-in-law, Sargent Shriver, who made it a reality.
77. Psalms 8: 4-5

Chapter 16
78. *Original Blessing,* Matthew Fox, Bear & Co., p. 184.
79. *Man and His Symbols,* Carl G. Jung, ed., Doubleday & Co., 1964, p. 152.
80. Luke 4: 18
81. John 14: 12-16
82. John 13: 34-35
83. John 17: 34-35
84. John 12: 32
85. Mark 12: 29-31

George Ritchie on videotape!

George Ritchie's experience inspired Dr. Ray Moody to begin the research that resulted in the best-selling book *Life After Life*. Now Dr. Moody's book has been made into a 57-minute color videotape, featuring gripping, first-person descriptions of the near-death experience by several of those who died and came back — including George Ritchie himself.

When Dr. Ritchie lent us his copy of the videotape, we liked it so much that we contacted the producer and arranged to offer it to our friends and readers.

This is no boring "talking heads" documentary. Instead, it is a fascinating exploration of all aspects of the near-death experience—including the all-important question of what it meant to those who had the experience! And the creative and imaginative use of video special effects dramatizes and adds impact to the descriptions.